PUTIN'S REAL INTENTIONS ON UKRAINE INVASION

HS PRESS

PUTIN'S REAL INTENTIONS ON UKRAINE INVASION

Interview with the President's Guardian Spirit

RYUHO OKAWA

HS PRESS

Copyright © 2022 by Ryuho Okawa
English translation © Happy Science 2022
Original title: *Ukraine Shinkou to Putin Daitoryou no Honshin*
HS Press is an imprint of IRH Press Co., Ltd.
Tokyo
ISBN 13: 978-1-943928-32-3
ISBN 10: 1-943928-32-0
Cover Image: EPA / PAVEL BEDNYAKOV / KREMLIN POOL / SPUTNIK

Contents

Preface 11

Putin's Real Intentions on Ukraine Invasion

1 Asking Putin's Guardian Spirit about the Situation of Ukraine and the Future

   The China-Russia problem foreseen for a decade is now a reality 18

   Did Russia and China discuss the Ukraine issue before the Beijing Olympics? 21

   The impact of sanctions on Russia and the outlook of the future 23

   Summoning President Putin's guardian spirit to ask him about his real intentions 25

2 Historical Background behind the Ukraine Problem

   Ryuho Okawa is the only Japanese who correctly understood the intent of the invasion of Crimea 27

   How do NATO and the EU look from Russia's side? 32

3 The Middle Ground of the Ukraine Issue

   How far does Putin aim to go with this Ukraine invasion? ... 36

   Displeased with how NATO is stubborn in their thinking, "Russia is the enemy" 38

   Thoughts on what would happen after, if sanctions are imposed 42

4 Honest Thoughts on Russia's Relationship with China

Putin's guardian spirit wants people to understand the differences between China and Russia 45

The Japanese do not understand Russia well 47

Putin's guardian spirit says, "Biden has no brains" 50

5 Frustrations with President Biden

How to read the future of the Biden administration 53

Why he says, "We don't need the EU or NATO" 55

What would be to Japan as Ukraine is to Russia? 58

The reason why Russia cannot attack China now 60

6 The Outlook on the Future of Japan, China, and Taiwan

What Xi Jinping asked of Putin at the Beijing Olympics 64

The prospects of the financial sanctions against Russia 68

Honest thoughts regarding the Four Northern Islands 70

7 The True Purpose of Invading Ukraine

Ukraine will only be sucked dry if it joins the EU 76

An anti-Russian NATO is not a pleasant thing to deal with 79

President Biden does not understand the significance of Ukraine 80

Revival of the Russian Empire is his dearest wish 83

His thoughts on Japan's position and China from now on 87

Why Putin's guardian spirit thinks the West is finished 90

Is God starting to choose which people to reduce? 94

8　Surprising Connections between Japan and Putin

What is the aim of Russia's "No evangelism outside of Church"? 96

From the Russian perspective, Japan appears to be a quasi-colony of the U.S. 98

Why Putin's guardian spirit is strongly interested in getting closer to Japan 101

Japan should be stronger and spread Japanese values ... 104

9　The Prospect of the World According to Putin's Guardian Spirit

China should take responsibility for spreading coronavirus around the world 107

How to deter China's military threats 108

Putin's guardian spirit encourages Japan to be neutral ... 112

One thing he would like to say about the virus 113

Can President Putin hear the voice of God? 115

10　You Cannot Rely Only on Information from the West to Understand the Situation in Ukraine 117

EXTRA CHAPTER

Spiritual Message from Ivan IV, the First Tsar of Russia
Ivan IV Talks about Russia's Struggle and the Drifting World

1 Ivan IV Appears, Fearing for the Future of Russia

  The spirit of the Russian Tsar suddenly appeared in the middle of the night 126

  Views on Russia's move to approach China 129

  The difference in the approach to Russia between Trump and Biden 136

2 Concerns about the Current Situation in Japan

  Wondering what Russia can do against China 141

  About the mission to make Russia strong 147

  Concerns about the situation Japan might have to face ... 149

3 Views on President Biden and the Coronavirus Pandemic

  Master Okawa's remark that gave hope to Ivan IV 152

  Talking about the impression of the Biden administration 156

  The culprit of spreading the novel coronavirus 160

4 About the Future of International Affairs
   Concerns that the entire world might drift 162
   Warning against Biden's foreign policy toward Asia 168

5 Thoughts on Russia's Relations with Japan and China
   Views on Iran and Israel 173
   The U.S. may drop off from being a superpower if it cannot fight back against China 177
   The mistake Japan was able to correct due to the coronavirus pandemic 179
   Thoughts on Japan's response to the Four Northern Islands, Takeshima, and Senkaku Islands 182
   What will become of the U.S. forces in Japan under the Biden administration? 185

Afterword 191

About the Author	193
What Is El Cantare?	194
What Is a Spiritual Message?	196
About Happy Science	200
Contact Information	202
About HS Press	204
Books by Ryuho Okawa	205
Music by Ryuho Okawa	215

Preface

The largest incident between Europe and Russia in 80 years is happening now.

Two nights ago, on the morning of February 24, I recorded the spiritual message about the Ukraine invasion and what President Putin's guardian spirit is thinking about. At that time, I still did not know of the Ukraine invasion by the Russian army, which started before dawn.

As of this writing, Russian forces are attacking Ukraine from three directions. One estimate has it that Ukraine lost control over its airspace in three hours. Russian tanks and military vehicles are advancing from the north, east, and south.

Japanese TV networks and national newspapers are denouncing Russia and calling the move "an act of aggression." American and European media outlets are doing largely the same.

It will begin with the economic sanctions from U.S. President Biden. Each nation of the G7, including Japan, will probably impose all kinds of sanctions on Russia.

War is a terrible thing, but we should see if there is justice in it.

Putin's proposals are 1) NATO must promise no further enlargement of the alliance to the east in a written document; 2) Do not deploy missile launchers to Poland or Romania; 3) Roll back NATO's strength to where it was in 1997. These were the three points, but the U.S. Biden administration rejected them.

President Zelensky in Kyiv is trying to take shelter in NATO, but President Putin could not possibly accept that.

It is not easy to develop an eye to see through international politics.

But one thing that's certain is that war would not have erupted in Ukraine if America had chosen Trump as president.

I deliver Mr. Putin's true thoughts to the people of Japan, who are insensitive to international matters, and to the rest of the world. It is worth getting a second opinion.

Ryuho Okawa
Master & CEO of Happy Science Group
February 26, 2022

These spiritual messages were channeled through Ryuho Okawa. However, please note that because of his high level of enlightenment, his way of receiving spiritual messages is fundamentally different from other psychic mediums who undergo trances and are completely taken over by the spirits they are channeling. When Master Okawa channels spirits who do not speak Japanese, they are sometimes able to use vocabulary from his language center to communicate their spiritual messages in Japanese.

Each human soul is generally made up of six soul siblings, one of whom acts as the guardian spirit of the person living on earth. People living on earth are connected to their guardian spirits at the innermost subconscious level. They are a part of people's very souls and, therefore, exact reflections of their thoughts and philosophies.

It should be noted that these spiritual messages are opinions of the individual spirits and may contradict the ideas or teachings of Happy Science Group.

Putin's Real Intentions on Ukraine Invasion

Originally recorded in Japanese on February 24, 2022
at the Special Lecture Hall of Happy Science in Japan
and later translated into English.

Vladimir Putin (1952 - Present)

A Russian politician. After graduating from the Faculty of Law of Leningrad State University, he worked for the former Soviet Union Committee for State Security [KGB]. He served as prime minister during the last days of the Yeltsin administration. He then became the president and served two terms (from 2000 to 2008) under the slogan, "Strong Russia." Afterward, he served as prime minister momentarily but returned to the presidency in March 2012. In March 2018, he won the election and is now serving the fourth presidential term.

He is pro-Japan and also known as a judo practitioner.

In this chapter, there are a total of three interviewers from Happy Science, symbolized as A, B, and C in the order that they first appear.

1

Asking Putin's Guardian Spirit about the Situation of Ukraine and the Future

The China-Russia problem foreseen for a decade is now a reality

RYUHO OKAWA

Good morning.

We have already published as many as five books of spiritual messages from the guardian spirit of Russian President Putin. I do not know if his books outnumbered the books of other spirits' messages, but once again, it

President Putin and the Future of Russia (Tokyo: HS Press, 2012)

A New Message from Vladimir Putin (Tokyo: HS Press, 2014)

Putin's Insights on Russia, Japan and the World (Tokyo: HS Press, 2016)

seems to be getting quite lively around him. As of now, his current action appears to be of a small scale, so on the one hand, I think it is better to wait and see how things go.

Looking at Mr. Putin as a politician, I think his surface consciousness or thoughts are highly in sync with his guardian spirit's thoughts. Unlike some other politicians who have the opposite thinking from their guardian spirits, about 80 percent of what Putin's guardian spirit says is consistent with the way of thinking of Putin himself.

As for the actual events, there are many media outlets that report them as they occur, and that is that. Although different people may have different interpretations, our mission is to ask his guardian spirit in advance to find out his intentions and use the information for future decisions and predictions. Then, we present our ideas on what course of action Japan and the international community should take. I think these are important.

I have been consistently insisting on separating Russia from China for the past 10 years, as there will be trouble if they form a military alliance. That is why I stressed the importance of Japan signing a peace treaty with Russia and preventing Russia from forming ties with China. I have warned of the threat to Japan if Russia should join hands with China. But since Mr. Abe (Japanese prime minister,

2012 – 2020) could not achieve it, I think it is even more difficult for Mr. Kishida (Japanese prime minister, 2021 – present) and other politicians.

What I fear now is the formation of alliances among Russia, China, North Korea, Iran, Pakistan, and some of the European countries. That could divide the world into two to create confrontations, resulting in quite a serious problem. We did what we could to prevent them from forming an alliance so that each county would be confronted separately, but sadly our efforts fell short of avoiding the current situation.

It seems to me that Mr. Biden is trying to start another world war, even though the world war is already happening with coronavirus. I wonder if he is going to take care of the two wars at the same time. I perceive him to be in a state of ignorance of the Truth, so he doesn't seem to know that.

The typical political formula would say that Japan will follow if the U.S. and Europe agree on something. So, it would be the usual course of events for Japan to join the trend of imposing international sanctions against Russia if it invades Ukraine, and even those who lack the ability to think will usually think so. However, we must analyze the future of world affairs more carefully at this stage.

Did Russia and China discuss the Ukraine issue before the Beijing Olympics?

RYUHO OKAWA

I am sure that before the Beijing Winter Olympics, Mr. Putin met with "that person" of China. I think they have already met almost 37 or 38 times. I recall Mr. Abe meeting with him just as many times.

I suspect they were coordinating the timing of the Winter Olympics and the military pressure on Ukraine. Coincidently, the current situation has given China a way out of public criticism. Prior to the Beijing Olympics, Russian troops began military exercises near Ukraine and took international attention away from China.

The United Nations (UN) had a plan to visit China, including the Xinjiang Uyghur Autonomous Region, for a full-scale hearing after the Winter Olympics. However, the current Russian military actions are preventing the hearing. At this point, Kremlin has officially recognized the independence of two breakaway regions in eastern Ukraine with a large ethnic Russian population after their leaders' request to protect those populations. It is a fine line whether to call their actions an invasion. However, the situation could escalate quickly. (Editor's note: On

February 24, at 6 a.m. <MSK time>, about two hours after this comment, President Putin gave an emergency speech, announcing he would launch special operations in eastern Ukraine. Then, a full-scale strike on Ukraine by the Russian army began.)

During the Winter Olympics, President Biden mentioned quite often that Putin would attack Kyiv, the capital of Ukraine, within days. I'm not sure how far they discussed it behind the scenes. In any case, it will become difficult to establish the world order after this. As far as I can see from various media outlets, they make no particular distinction between Russia and China.

It is said that Russia will invade Ukraine this month, February 2022. In 2014, Russia suddenly invaded Crimea, which drew condemnation from Europe. Previously in 2008, Russia entered the area of Georgia with a large ethnic Russian population on the pretext of their protection. The two incidents occurred in 2008 and 2014, leading up to the current event.

The impact of sanctions on Russia and the outlook of the future

RYUHO OKAWA

The international response will be led by financial sanctions from the U.S. against Russia to prevent Mr. Putin, his entourage, and their families from accessing their assets. It will prevent Russia from raising funds abroad. The U.K. has already implemented economic sanctions, and Mr. Kishida is working on similar measures—disallowing Russia to raise funds by the issue of government bonds in Japan.

In Germany, Ms. Merkel retired, and a new chancellor has been appointed. For them, the biggest issue with Russia is the natural gas pipeline. It is clear that once the war breaks out, the pipeline will not be able to function. Still, the new chancellor quickly halted the gas pipeline project, and in the meantime, the U.S. tankers carrying liquefied natural gas had already arrived in Europe.

However, in reality, inflation in fuel prices has already begun in Europe. Electricity and gas prices have tripled or quadrupled in some areas, putting pressure on the economy. It seems that Italy is making adjustments to save money, like cooking spaghetti more carefully and lowering the thermostat down to 15 degrees Celsius at night.

Well, how long could this situation last? What is going to happen?

What about the cooperation between Russia and China? How about the threat of North Korea and China's hypersonic missiles, which apparently have capabilities of flying at Mach 5 to 10? Coincidently, Russia has also mentioned its hypersonic missiles. I do not know whether these countries have a connection, but the U.S. does not have this technology yet. It is unknown what would happen if these weapons were put to use.

It seems that Mr. Biden is going to take measures little by little to keep Russia in check. I am not sure how broad Biden's perspective is.

The other thing is that Mr. Biden's strong desire to attack Russia arising from his competition against Mr. Trump is still driving him. I suspect Mr. Biden is trying to create a thorough bad impression of any ties to Russia in order to prevent Mr. Trump from regaining his power. As a result, the U.S. is giving China an advantage while pretending to threaten them.

This is my impression of the situation.

Summoning President Putin's guardian spirit to ask him about his real intentions

RYUHO OKAWA

[*To the interviewers.*] Since we are already familiar with Mr. Putin's guardian spirit, I hope your tactful interview skills can reveal his real intentions. Japan is not yet in a position to go to war, so please find out what he is thinking about. From a journalistic view, discovering his thought process or interviewing and presenting facts alone can be good enough. The issue is what people make of the information.

Our organization has no real power to deal with this issue, so we cannot take any action. However, finding out what is on the mind of Russia's top leader itself is meaningful. I don't know how Japan's Prime Minister's Office would deal with this information, but I think the Ministry of Defense and the Self-Defense Forces will find our information useful.

Now, let's get started.

I would like to call upon the guardian spirit of Mr. Vladimir Putin, the president of Russia, who is currently grabbing headlines worldwide, to come to Happy Science again.

President Putin's guardian spirit, President Putin's guardian spirit.

Please come down to Happy Science and share your opinion regarding the current disputes and what may become problematic in the future.

Please share your thoughts.

[*About five seconds of silence.*]

2
Historical Background behind the Ukraine Problem

Ryuho Okawa is the only Japanese who correctly understood the intent of the invasion of Crimea

PUTIN'S GUARDIAN SPIRIT
Hmm.

INTERVIEWER A
Hello. Are you the guardian spirit of President Putin?

PUTIN'S G.S.
Yes.

A
Thank you very much for your time today.

PUTIN'S G.S.
You guys should've worked harder. Things are beginning to go wrong in the world.

A

Tension is now mounting in Ukraine in February 2022.

PUTIN'S G.S.

I'll be around until about 2036. Yes.

A

Thank you for this opportunity to speak with you. The situation in Ukraine is now in chaos, but the Western media has taken an extremely strong tone of condemnation, saying President Putin is attempting to change the status quo by force. Japanese media is also following suit.

We would appreciate it if you could tell us how you see the situation involving Ukraine as well as the world from Russia's point of view.

PUTIN'S G.S.

Russian people are giving me a loud, heartfelt applause.

A

Yes.

PUTIN'S G.S.

People are giving me a standing ovation. The bottom line is that they had lost their country. The Soviet Union, which was a huge nation, broke apart and dissolved into pieces during the times of Gorbachev and Yeltsin. Only Russia remained, and the rest became independent.

Also, the EU is using its power to slowly invade us further.

I know many people suspect that I have the vision to build a great Russian empire. Even if I don't go that far, I think some of the critical areas for the future of Russia must be recovered.

When we started entering Crimea in 2014, the only Japanese who understood our true intention was Mr. Ryuho Okawa.

A

Yes.

PUTIN'S G.S.

The base of Russia's Black Sea Fleet is in Crimea, so if we don't keep hold of that area, we can't use the fleet. It will make our defense extremely vulnerable. It means if Russia is attacked from the EU or the U.S. side, whether we can use the Black Sea Fleet or not will make a big difference.

What's left are the Arctic Ocean side and [*extending his right arm*] the Sakhalin side in Siberia.

Russia is confined within a world of snow and ice more than you might think. So, I welcome global warming. [*Laughs.*] It will make us more affluent and open access to the surrounding areas. Since our country is ice- and snow-bound, we must constantly secure our route for security reasons.

That's why we had to keep the Black Sea Fleet in Crimea, even if we were condemned. Ukraine is an extension of that strategy.

Ukraine is a rather large country, probably the second-largest country in Europe. It is also the breadbasket, so if the EU takes this region, it is as if Japan had lost Kyushu, Hokkaido, Ou, and Shikoku regions to the allied forces after the defeat in World War II, and those areas were made to become independent as republics. The collapse of the Soviet Union can be explained like this.

Imagine having only the Kanto region around Tokyo remain as Japan. Well, Japan is smaller than Russia, but that is our current situation. If Ukraine should become independent and join the EU, it would be like Kanagawa Prefecture (next to Tokyo) becoming the Republic of

Kanagawa and getting closer to the U.S. or China or some other places. So, think about the danger of Kanagawa having ties with the country that is threatening Tokyo. I hope this helps you to imagine the current situation.

A
Now, U.S. President Biden is trying to impose economic sanctions. To put it simply, he is portraying President Putin as the bad dictator in Russia who is trying to disrupt the world order.

PUTIN'S G.S.
[*Smiles wryly.*]

A
Such stories are made...

PUTIN'S G.S.
I've been the leader since 2000, so it makes me one of the longest-reigning leaders. Russia has the most outstanding leader. To be honest, the U.S. should have such a leader, but it is difficult for someone to remain the president over there. The administration changes here and there.

A

On the other hand, Mr. Trump has recently said that Mr. Putin is a genius.

PUTIN'S G.S.

Yes. We both think so. It takes a genius to recognize one. No matter how much time passes, ordinary people won't understand. They cannot tell the difference.

How do NATO and the EU look from Russia's side?

A

Let me ask first specifically about the situation of Ukraine. President Putin has long said that he must prevent NATO from expanding eastward and that Russia will be in trouble if Ukraine should join NATO.

PUTIN'S G.S.

NATO must be destroyed. It's against God's Will. A bunch of stupid people gathered around and made a coalition of the weak. They need to stop dragging the world down with them. Obviously, there is no leader.

Stop dragging the whole of Europe from around Belgium. It doesn't make sense. What would they know being in such a small place like that? It's really annoying.

NATO, at first, was a military organization of the EU but more toward the U.S. But the EU was originally designed to compete against Japan. The EU was created because Japan became too powerful and was about to overtake the U.S. None of the European countries could win against Japan either: that's why they all gathered to counter Japan. The EU was really made to go against Japan.

But Japan fell on its own, and thanks to the 30 years of stagnation, it was no longer the enemy. The EU then looked for the next enemy, saw Russia reviving, and decided to throw a punch.

So it means I've been very successful in the economic recovery and the restoration of national power over the last 20 years.

A

In terms of Ukraine, after the political upheaval in 2014 when the pro-Russian President Yanukovych was ousted, the country almost took a pro-Western course. But because the pro-Russian forces were within the two eastern regions, in 2015, the Minsk Agreements were made. Although

Germany, France, Ukraine, and Russia were almost settled on a plan to meet on the same page, the fact that this plan has not been implemented became the direct trigger now for Russia.

But on the other hand, President Biden has taken a very hardline stance against Russia.

PUTIN'S G.S.
That's right. Biden is trying to gain approval ratings.

A
Perhaps, it seems more like the U.S. is provoking Russia rather than Russia being aggressive.

PUTIN'S G.S.
Yes, that's right. The U.S. is the one who's provoking.

Since competing against Trump in the presidential election, many pieces of information have been released about Russia, like the possibility of Russian cyber-attacks and Russian money flow.

Even now, the media seems to be trying hard to report that Russian cyber-attacks are about to hit the whole world. I won't do such a thing. If I were to make a move, I'd fire missiles directly. I won't be so roundabout like that.

Well, if Russia did cyber... Cyber-attacks are effective if people don't know who did them. Once people know, there's no point.

Nothing good comes out of the whole world becoming confused and communication being shut down. If I'm going to make a move, I'm going to do it clearly.

3

The Middle Ground of the Ukraine Issue

How far does Putin aim to go with this Ukraine invasion?

A

What is the middle ground for now, or how far do you aim to go? Although I understand you may not reveal all since the state of conflict is approaching.

PUTIN'S G.S.

I want the eastern and southern parts of Ukraine. Then I will settle things this time.

Because I don't think we can get rid of all of them from Ukraine. I cannot just give the whole of Ukraine to the EU. As Master Okawa once said, if American nuclear weapons and missiles were lined up there, Russia would become completely defenseless. Within 10 minutes, Moscow would be destroyed.

If someone weaker than me becomes president, it could be the end of Russia. So while I am still here, a decision must absolutely be made.

INTERVIEWER B
If you're asking for the east and south of Ukraine, then you've almost achieved your goal at this point...

PUTIN'S G.S.
No, I haven't achieved it yet. Not yet. I will do a little more.

B
A little more?

PUTIN'S G.S.
A little more. It's not enough. They might fight back.

B
With the current stance of President Putin, the U.S. and NATO probably can't put any more military pressure despite their talks. It seems like that's the case as long as you don't start an action. So I think what you should have is pretty much in your pocket.

PUTIN'S G.S.
Britain should just be quiet since they left the EU, but why is Johnson, the baldy, trying so hard?

Displeased with how NATO is stubborn in their thinking, "Russia is the enemy"

B
You mentioned earlier that NATO and the EU must be destroyed because their mission is over. This is extremely interesting.

PUTIN'S G.S.
They're not needed.

B
They're not needed?

PUTIN'S G.S.
Not needed. Because they don't have the enemy, Japan. Only Russia is left.

B

At the beginning of this session, Master Okawa said that the opinions of the guardian spirit and President Putin himself on earth match about 80 percent or more. Does that mean what you said is the real intention of President Putin, and he really is thinking that far?

PUTIN'S G.S.

If NATO is dealing with, for example, China and North Korea, then I think it's fair, but they're not thinking about that. So, the enemy is only Russia. The way they think hasn't changed since the Napoleonic Wars.

B

I think that your logic is very clear and easy to understand, and you are also a very honest person.

PUTIN'S G.S.

Yes. During the time of the Great Soviet Union, the land was 61 times larger than that of Japan. If the leader were like Stalin, of course, Europe would need to unite to protect itself. But I'm a gentleman; even my wife left me. So you don't have to worry.

B

So does that mean, once you have a hold of a part of Ukraine, there will be an armistice?

PUTIN'S G.S.

No, I don't care about Ukraine. What's important is to make sure that there is no flashpoint for war.

B

So, that's how you will settle. Then, historically speaking, do you think NATO and the EU are no longer necessary?

PUTIN'S G.S.

Don't you think the EU is a coalition of the weak?

B

Yes.

PUTIN'S G.S.

Britain left, and also, Germany and France don't get along, so they can't be united anyway. Germany is getting nuclear power from France, but it's also pulling a natural gas pipeline from Russia so that it won't become under the control of France. Germany was trying to make itself independent by getting energy from both sides. They have the negative carry-over from Merkel's era and how she also overfed China in some ways. That's why things need to be changed, but the current one (Chancellor Scholz) is not very smart either.

B

You seem to be thinking on a worldwide scale. Looking at what's really happening on earth today, I think there will be politicians in the world who would feel extremely nervous when hearing your real intentions.

PUTIN'S G.S.

I'd think so. The same goes for Japan.

B

How to make these ends meet...

PUTIN'S G.S.

I don't know. Japan's stance is like, "If the West says so, then it must be." Biden is saying it is democracies versus autocracies, but why should Biden decide? Why should the world move according to what the U.S. says?

If you look at what the U.S. has been doing for a long time, there are some good things, but there are also a lot of bad things. The desert area was attacked hard, so was Vietnam, there was also the Korean War, and Japan is how it is now. It's a country that needs to atone for its deeds once and for all. That's why it shouldn't have so much power. It's time for the U.S. to become just another country like the rest.

Thoughts on what would happen after, if sanctions are imposed

INTERVIEWER C
The U.S. has said that they will impose unprecedented economic sanctions on Russia.

PUTIN'S G.S.
That old man speaks nonsense.

C
But I believe you are taking measures, already factoring in such sanctions.

PUTIN'S G.S.
Well, for me, both Russia and China have a certain amount of land. So we can survive. I think we'll manage food and fuel so we will be OK.

"Unprecedented"? The U.S. will just gradually lose trading partners, poor them. Actually, I think there should be a retirement age for the U.S. president.

B
As expected, Mr. Biden can't keep up with President Putin's big initiative. So he started being peevish, saying this and that. If this is your real intention, I really feel that a person like Mr. Biden might just faint or would almost snap.

PUTIN'S G.S.
Then so be it. If his blood vessels in the brain snap, he would actually contribute to world peace.

B
Is that so?

PUTIN'S G.S.

He's the kind of person who should just be around in Khrushchev's time.

B

I think that kind of thinking is what makes the world probably a little scared of President Putin.

PUTIN'S G.S.

Depending on the case, I didn't mind returning the Four Northern Islands (to Japan), but the U.S. did something like this.

The U.S. used NATO to attack Russia.

Now, there are Russian military bases in the two big islands of the Four Northern Islands. If we return the four islands in a situation like this, the U.S. will then build military bases there. With the idea of attacking Russia from Siberia, we will be attacked from both sides. We really don't want this pattern of events, so we can't return these islands even if we wanted to.

4

Honest Thoughts on Russia's Relationship with China

Putin's guardian spirit wants people to understand the differences between China and Russia

A

While the Ukraine situation is happening, recently, there have been military exercises in the Northern Territories. Last autumn (2021), during the Japanese lower house elections, naval vessels from China and Russia jointly circled the Japanese archipelago. We know President Putin has met with Xi Jinping at the Beijing Olympics, and I'd like to ask you about how you see the world situation now while keeping your eyes on Ukraine. Especially regarding the Far East.

PUTIN'S G.S.

There is a famous proverb, "The enemy of my enemy is my friend," which is the extent of our relationship. We're not that close [*laughs*]. We don't really get along, but if an enemy appears, you have to make the enemy of your enemy your friend in terms of the military as well. This is the thinking of Carl Schmitt.

We don't like China that much. We are like enemies who just happen to be in the same boat. But if the West were to attack us, we would have to help each other.

A

Mr. Trump has praised President Putin as a genius and has also warned about the imminent invasion of Taiwan.

PUTIN'S G.S.

Yes, well, I bet that's what he is afraid of at the same time. If our activities are used as camouflage or a diversion, people will not know even if China were to enter Taiwan. Because people are so focused on Europe, and if Biden keeps saying Russia is the villain, people may consider Ukraine as the bigger problem and think, "Taiwan is small. Never mind about Taiwan; we can deal with that later."

But the difference in thinking is that we are doing this partly because we need to protect some of the ethnic Russians who are being oppressed there. The country was once part of the Soviet Union and then became independent. So, I'd like you to know that there is a difference between us protecting the Russians who were originally in our country and China oppressing the Tibetans, Uyghurs, and Mongolians and trying to take Taiwan.

The Japanese do not understand Russia well

B
Japan, including us, is focusing on Russia's relationship with China. I think many people are wondering whether you are starting to lose patience because despite being tolerant for a long time, the response from the U.S. and Japanese governments has been extremely poor.

PUTIN'S G.S.
Hmm.

B
I mean the response against China.

PUTIN'S G.S.
The Japanese don't understand Russia well. I guess it may be because the Russian language is difficult. Even so, about 80 percent of Russian people are pro-Japanese; we

have become pro-Japanese after losing our war with Japan. Perhaps Japan has also become more pro-American after losing to the U.S.

Currently, we have to make friends even with neighboring countries that are not so good for Japan in order to maintain the country. Also, we will deepen our relationship with anti-American countries in Central and South America. The closer a country is to the U.S., the more they hate the United States. Countries far away cannot understand this, but close countries can understand it very well. Anyway, Central and South America are against the U.S. By strengthening our relations with them, it will be like the world of... I don't know if this is more like chess, *go*, or Japanese *shogi*, but it will be a battle of wits.

B

In that case, from the outside, your actions will look very similar to what China is doing, so I think people around the world will likely get suspicious.

PUTIN'S G.S.

I guess so.

So, people are getting confused, and Europe doesn't really understand China. They may very well be thinking of Japan as a province of China. That is the extent of their understanding. It's the same in the U.S. It is unclear to Mr. Biden as well; the Asian region looks obscure. If the U.S. drew the old map of the Flat Earth model from their perspective, Japan would be on edge near a waterfall. They don't actually see you.

B

Based on what you said, it seems like President Putin has a broader perspective and doesn't care about Russia being perceived in such a way.

PUTIN'S G.S.

We're both superpowers, so the question of what's right and wrong doesn't matter so much anymore when we've come this far. The one with true power wins. That's it. If you don't have true power, you'll lose.

The survival of our nation is on the line. If Europe and the U.S. impose sanctions on us and other countries also follow suit, trying to contain Russia by leaving us to "starve," a system to "bully Russia" will be created. On top of that, if China starts praising Biden as a "good person" and sends bribes to him to besiege Russia, then everything will be over for us.

Putin's guardian spirit says, "Biden has no brains"

B

But, according to the news this morning, they were speculating that the financial sanctions were actually being imposed carefully so as not to wake the sleeping giant, President Putin, and to prevent it from becoming fatal. It seems like the West stopped imposing further sanctions on Russia after that. I think they thought this out.

PUTIN'S G.S.

Well, they may think they've avoided waking the sleeping giant, but they've definitely woken him up. It's beyond insulting. They deserve to be struck back.

B

I know it's insulting, but... they are trying to maintain the situation from escalating too far and stopping it from turning into a war.

PUTIN'S G.S.
It's like foreigners passing in front of a *daimyo* procession. They should be executed, much like how the Namamugi Incident[1] happened.

B
Seeing President Putin living on earth, he seems to be thinking very carefully about the way he sends out his troops and his opening moves so that it is difficult for the other side to respond. Even regarding the U.S., leaving Mr. Biden aside, the people under him are probably working on trying and keeping the other side in check so as not to irritate Mr. Putin too much.

PUTIN'S G.S.
Those are the mass media's predictions, but it's not like that. They are not thinking about such things because they are simple-minded. They aren't thinking—they aren't thinking at all...

B
That's the idea you have, judging from the situation.

PUTIN'S G.S.

Biden has no brains.

About 75 percent of our military is positioned around Ukraine. If we want to take the country, we can. So the question is, "To what extent do they want us to hold back?"

5

Frustrations with President Biden

How to read the future of the Biden administration

A

As an explanation for why you decided to make the moves you did, some think it's because you have judged President Biden as incompetent after meeting directly with him last June. Others think it's because you have judged the Biden administration as weak after seeing the shameful withdrawal of the U.S. from Afghanistan in August. People think maybe that's why you took such bold moves. The Biden administration is scheduled to continue for the next three years. I'd like to know how you see this situation.

PUTIN'S G.S.

It's like asking you, an outstanding person, what it would be like if you were to study at a slow-paced local university and learn the same thing you studied again for another four years. You would probably go out to the ocean and start surfing or snorkeling in the middle of your studies, and you would stop attending classes. This is the extent of boredom I feel when I talk to Biden.

B

So, you're essentially saying you've had enough.

PUTIN'S G.S.

We don't have time to deal with such an idiot. I wonder how such a man managed to pull through. Aren't there any other capable people in the U.S.?

A

Conversely, one could also see this as an opportunity for Russia.

PUTIN'S G.S.

I've been part of world history and have been in power for over 20 years.

Why he says,
"We don't need the EU or NATO"

C
President Biden said it is a battle of autocracies versus democracies.

PUTIN'S G.S.
What is he talking about?! He means "versus nations without leadership," right?

C
Master Ryuho Okawa does not see it that way. He sees that it should be a great conflict between countries with faith and countries without faith.

PUTIN'S G.S.
So, you know, there's something wrong. Christian countries are often at war. We have to ask if they are actually Christians or not. Don't you think Christian countries are often at war? This doesn't seem right.

C

President Putin seems to think he has to prevent his country from becoming materialist.

PUTIN'S G.S.

Yes. So, you don't need the EU or NATO or anything like that. The world should just listen to El Cantare (see back page). Then, it will all be resolved. You don't need them. Even if idiots get together and have a meeting, idiots will still be idiots!

B

Your logic is very clear, and the conclusion is correct, but there will probably be many people who cannot approve of your actual process...

PUTIN'S G.S.

The world should only read your magazine, *The Liberty*.

B

It's a matter of how to persuade and organize such countries...

PUTIN'S G.S.
Such countries are unnecessary!

B
"Unnecessary" [*laughs*].

PUTIN'S G.S.
Such idiots are unnecessary! We don't need them. Idiots who are below average should just stay put. There is just no need for them to attend global meetings.

B
You are being quite straightforward with your words.

PUTIN'S G.S.
I'm just a little more irritated than usual. It's getting to me.

B
I see.

PUTIN'S G.S.
I'm furious. I honestly can't stand this without having some vodka and getting drunk. We have a lot, so I want

to launch them already! That's how I actually feel, but I'm trying to be patient. I'm going along with these pointless talks... Idiots! I can't take such idiots seriously. Alumni of the University of Tokyo need to work a little harder. Really. Those idiots... [*Shakes his head from side to side.*] Japan is sinking because such intelligent people are regarded the same as many others by society. Elites must follow the true path of the elite, really.

What would be to Japan as Ukraine is to Russia?

C
President Putin himself has said something like the ethnic Russians in Donetsk and Luhansk are being massacred and that genocide is taking place.

PUTIN'S G.S.
Well, that might be true. It could happen. They are certainly bombarding each other. So, if nothing is done, they will lose because the Ukrainian army is stronger. There is no way to protect the local Russians. Before all of this started, Russia had actually already provided military support. But

well, this is all too much fuss, so I am deciding whether to just take over Ukraine or not. We can if we want to. If you say it's OK, we'll take it!

B
Well, how do I put it… this spiritual message will probably be published, so with that in mind… what you are saying makes a lot of sense, but you are presenting ideas that will probably take three to five years for people in this world to understand.

PUTIN'S G.S.
Hmm.

B
In other words, your comments are satisfying but, at the same time, could lead to further confusion in the actual world. This is what I am thinking about as I ask you questions.

PUTIN'S G.S.
Well, we are a worm-eaten state. If you are told Tokyo and Osaka belong to Japan, but Nagoya and the Chubu region

belong to other places, how do you expect the bullet train to run? That's how it feels from our point of view. The EU is an alliance of the weak. There are only a few decent nations. It's mostly just France and Germany making the decisions, right? Even so, the leaders are not that great.

The reason why Russia cannot attack China now

B
If you keep insisting on that, the world will continue to be in chaos or confusion and, in some ways, enter a time of conflict.

PUTIN'S G.S.
You know what, I can hear God's voice. I can hear the voice telling me to reduce the population...

B
Oh, I see. It's as if you're playing a part in it in some way...

PUTIN'S G.S.
I've been thinking, I can help.

B
Ah, so you're thinking of helping.

PUTIN'S G.S.
I'm thinking of which country I should start with, in reducing the population. I can help with that. Even when China is scattering the virus, the idiot Biden is... Eight million people are already infected, and how many died? Oh, not eight million; I meant 80 million. Eighty million people are already infected, and over 900,000 have died (in the U.S.). Even though this is all China's doing, why on earth is he attacking us instead of China? That fool.

A
As you just said, if this is indeed a coronavirus war on the macro level, why are they (the U.S.) instigating the conflict in Ukraine when instead, the attacks should be directed at China?

PUTIN'S G.S.
Right. In Russia, tens of millions are infected. Already over 20 million people? Tens of millions are already infected, and it has recently been disclosed that the death

toll is actually double the announced number; they said our death toll is twice what we announced and that Russia actually has the second-largest death toll in the world. Well, I suppose it is true [*laughs*]. If people know too much about such information, it becomes difficult for the government to maintain its power, so most governments tend to announce numbers smaller than they actually are. We're suffering a lot of damage, so it's obvious that we didn't do it. Russia was not involved in the spread of the viruses.

It's natural to be suspicious of a big country with little damage. A detective, or anyone, will come to that same conclusion. It's just impossible. That country (China) should have tens of millions of infected people. If not, it's bizarre. So, you can only assume that the pandemic was planned by that country.

C
Are you going to do something to retaliate against China?

PUTIN'S G.S.
So, first, if Russia is going to be attacked from the outside, then we have to use China until that point. After that,

we can help sort out China. But if Russia is going to be attacked now, we can't attack China.

China probably did it (spread the coronavirus), but Biden can't prove it because doing so means he'll have to pay the price for receiving bribes as well. In any case, Biden is probably trying to make Russia the villain so that he can complete his presidential term. But there's no way out. It's already clear that his son took bribes. While he's in power, he probably won't be impeached, but it will be a tragedy when he does get ousted. It won't be a surprise if he gets arrested. But all he has been doing is raising questions against Trump. So, I think the U.S. and its citizens have become cold toward the two-party system. They are probably wondering if this is the right way to go.

6

The Outlook on the Future of Japan, China, and Taiwan

What Xi Jinping asked of Putin at the Beijing Olympics

A

It seems like demonizing Russia can distract us from the real enemy. What do you think about that?

PUTIN'S G.S.

Well, I think Xi Jinping is trying to use Russia. We know that. I will let them use us, but I have to use them as well. If China shows alarming activities, the U.S. will also have to act on that. In that case, they will have to engage in a two-front operation, and their forces will be divided. So it means attacking Russia would supposedly lead China to start its action.

A

The dangerous thing with the U.S. foreign policy is that the U.S. is motioning toward intervening in Ukraine when it should be focusing on China. Biden is exaggerating and saying World War III will begin if the U.S. intervenes.

PUTIN'S G.S.
World War III has already begun. It has already started.

A
Right.

PUTIN'S G.S.
I want to say to him, "How can you still not realize when nearly a million of your own people were killed? Are you that stupid?"

If we start a full-scale war in Ukraine, and at the same time, China launches a surprise attack on Taiwan, will the U.S. fight against both countries while imposing sanctions on them? Ha [*laughs*]. That will be interesting. Let's see if he can actually do it. Both of us have hypersonic missiles. And North Korea will probably join the war as well. Interesting. I bet there will be missiles flying all over the world.

A
Speaking of the Far East, how do you view North Korea's consecutive missile tests in January of this year?

PUTIN'S G.S.
They're linked.

A
Yes.

PUTIN'S G.S.
In order to prevent the world from condemning China for human rights issues at the Beijing Olympics, North Korea was shooting missiles and attracting attention as a diversion. Russia is also drawing attention by gathering troops. Xi Jinping asked us to do this.

A
I see.

PUTIN'S G.S.
We were asked not to let the whole world focus on China-bashing... Going to see the Uyghur region is no longer the priority for the Secretary-General of the UN. Their issue now is the European crisis.

C

So, President Putin is doing what he is doing while knowing all this.

PUTIN'S G.S.

That's right. But the enemy of an enemy is a friend, so we will both use each other while we can. When our interests don't align, we will clash with each other. It can't be helped.

A

As for the background of what's happening in Ukraine, although it was different during the Trump era, the U.S. has been trying to get into the Russian sphere of interest and intervene for a long time. This was also true during the political upheaval in Ukraine.

PUTIN'S G.S.

That's right. That's what is going on. They're interfering. Mr. Trump would have been able to read my thoughts. If Trump were president of Russia, he'd probably do the same thing I did. I can tell. He would think of the same thing.

The prospects of the financial sanctions against Russia

A

As a means to push Russia further into a corner in the future, financial sanctions are on the table. The first step of these sanctions is going on now, but there is also a possibility of Russia being excluded from the dollar payment system. This could be very damaging for Russia. What do you think about that?

PUTIN'S G.S.

Hmm. Well, I doubt it will be that bad.

A

You don't think it will get to that point?

PUTIN'S G.S.

Right. Given the top two leaders of the U.S., they will only hasten the decline of their own country.

B

So, you don't expect them to exercise their power to that extent?

PUTIN'S G.S.
After all, they don't understand anything. They are empty-headed, really.

A
The people working under Biden are...

PUTIN'S G.S.
But the people under him are smarter—smarter than average. But if the top is incompetent, then it's helpless. There is no way to even make him seem like a good leader.

A
Do you mean, even if the people below him were to scheme a plot, it wouldn't be successful?

PUTIN'S G.S.
At the cabinet-level or strategy-making level, some under him are close to your level of intelligence. But the two at the top are boneheads, so it's helpless. The American people are already waiting for them to die. And, there's no need for a vice president whose approval rating dropped to the 20 percent range within a year. I bet people are

hoping that she drowns somewhere or is killed in a drone attack. I really think so.

Honest thoughts regarding the Four Northern Islands

A
As for Japan, Mr. Abe tried to make progress on the ongoing dispute regarding the Northern Territories, but...

PUTIN'S G.S.
Well, I will ultimately use that as a bargaining chip, too. Suppose the moron Biden's strategy pans out, causing Russia to "starve" on its own, and the world condemns Russia and wishes for me to die on the guillotine. In that case, I might be willing to bet on Japan to open a passage to Japan in exchange for the Four Northern Islands. But it depends on who the Japanese prime minister is.

A
Right. If the one who receives the message in Japan is...

PUTIN'S G.S.
If the prime minister can't make decisions, this plan won't work.

A
At the moment, the negotiations Mr. Abe had with Russia may have completely been reset.

PUTIN'S G.S.
It didn't work. He was in office for nine years, so I thought he would have had a little more strength, but he couldn't do anything. He couldn't make amends to the constitution nor conclude a peace treaty with Russia. There was no progress.

And if he had nine years, he should have made nuclear missiles. Why didn't he make any? I bet he knows deep down that he should have. Surviving by hiding one's true feelings is disgraceful. He doesn't even deserve the title of samurai. He should say what he wants to say. Only Happy Science is speaking its mind. The Happiness Realization Party speaks its mind and isn't getting enough votes.

It's because the mass media has it all wrong. The left-wing media... After World War II, all the mass media companies essentially bowed down and said, "We are sorry for what we did before the war. Please let us live." They have all taken an oath behind the scenes. That's why they don't touch on that at all. It's about time a revolution started in Japan. You have a chance while I'm still alive. I can't help you after that.

A
I see. I think you had a lot of expectations for us.

PUTIN'S G.S.
I want to open the route to Japan. If it opens up... In other words, if we don't open a route to the sea, we will be trapped in case of a critical situation. It's all frozen ground here. We're in the snow. If Japan opens up to us, we can connect with the world. I think it makes a big difference. I'm in a position to make this kind of decision. It's a privilege of being a "dictator." Unlike the U.S., this is the good part of Russia—I can make such decisions if I want to.

The Japanese public opinion and mass media are following the West's lead. So, Mr. Ryuho Okawa is the only one who can criticize the mass media. Nothing can be done in this given situation. Why don't you, Japan, just close the Diet? I don't think it's necessary. Need approval for the budget? All they do is create a budget that results in a budget deficit. Who cares? They keep doing useless things. Stop pouring money into healthcare and instead charge China. That is the reason why your healthcare is in a critical situation, right? Ridiculous.

A
So, you are saying President Putin wishes for a strong Japan.

PUTIN'S G.S.
Yes. In the end, I'd like to keep the Japanese route open. If I am checkmated, there may be no way out, so I ultimately want to keep the Japanese route open. I don't care about the Four Northern Islands; to be honest, it doesn't really matter. But there have been military bases on the islands since Medvedev's time. It's part of our preparations in case the U.S. invades; there is a possibility of them coming in through Siberia. That's why we cannot return the islands now. If our relations with Japan improve...

How should we deal with the U.S.? I'd like to see the U.S. properly settle their post-World War II deeds once and for all.

A

What is your prediction on what will happen if Xi Jinping actually takes military action against Taiwan? This involves Japan, even though it may be a very unlikely scenario.

PUTIN'S G.S.

Well, I don't know. I'm not even sure what I would say because...

A

Given how weak President Biden is, it's unclear how far he will go...

PUTIN'S G.S.

I don't know if it's Xi Jinping's real intention, but he mentioned things that made it sound like he was not so supportive of our annexation of Crimea as well as the establishment of independent separatist regions in the eastern part of Ukraine that we are doing now. I don't know his real intention, though. He probably intends to do something similar, but I don't know. I don't know if he wants to be lumped together with us or not. China might say, "Taiwan was originally China's territory and is an internal affair, so it is different from the Ukraine issue." They may also say, "Russia even tried to invade a foreign country," and frame it in such a light.

7

The True Purpose of Invading Ukraine

Ukraine will only be sucked dry if it joins the EU

B

From the perspective of the U.S. not having to engage in a two-front operation, if Russia stops at the eastern and southern fronts of Ukraine, the U.S. would be able to maintain security in both Europe and Taiwan because they would not have to concentrate their forces in Europe. In other words, Russia invading Ukraine as a whole would escalate the situation enough so that the U.S. would have to make a move.

So, if you were to take an aggressive approach which you are speaking of now... Well, I understand my main role today is to ask you questions, but if I may make a request or a plea, once you've held down the southern and eastern parts, perhaps you accomplished your original goal, so could you...

PUTIN'S G.S.
In any case, I'd like to secure a route to the Black Sea. If this area is blocked, the only way out will be near the Baltic States. And after that, the Four Northern Islands will be in danger. There is also a possibility of the U.S. attacking there, so it is a bit dangerous.

But I think the Ukrainian people are being deceived as well. They think that a golden future awaits them in the EU, but I think they are being deceived. The EU is in trouble right now. There are a lot of Muslims pouring in, and everyone is finding it troublesome. The EU is becoming economically poor, and they are not doing so well. So, the EU actually doesn't want to accept any more refugees.

B
Right. After listening to you this time, I understand very well that President Putin's sense of justice actually expands to Europe and also to the western half of Ukraine, and this is what lies behind his strong claims regarding this.

PUTIN'S G.S.
So, I think it would probably be better for Ukraine to join Russia instead. If they join the EU, they will probably just be sucked dry. There won't be anything good, really.

They may think they will get financial aid, but the EU won't be able to provide it. Europe is trying to get rid of some countries. Since Merkel's time, they've been trying to get rid of all the bad debt-like countries, like Italy and Greece, and China was trying to "eat them up." If Ukraine thinks it could get a "blood transfusion," they are sorely mistaken. The EU will probably just take advantage of the good parts of Ukraine.

C

President Zelensky of Ukraine became popular on TV and then became president. From President Putin's point of view, does he appear to be someone with no sense of judgment?

PUTIN'S G.S.

Well, he certainly doesn't see the world. He can only see his own country. He only cares about staying in power... I've been doing this long enough that I can see the world. So...

Putin's Real Intentions on Ukraine Invasion

An anti-Russian NATO is not a pleasant thing to deal with

C

Regarding NATO, do you think it must disappear?

PUTIN'S G.S.

What is the purpose of NATO, anyway?

C

You're thinking, "How far will they expand before they are satisfied?"

PUTIN'S G.S.

Now, it basically exists to counter Russia, right? I am not sure if there are 30 member-states or more, but if they all get together and unite against Russia, it would be unbearable for us. We must do something to inhibit this... anyone would do the same thing.

C

When Germany was reunified, President Gorbachev made a verbal agreement with the then U.S. president, George H.

W. Bush, that NATO would not accept any more member countries, but there was no written agreement...

PUTIN'S G.S.
We've been saying that, too, but they don't seem to understand what it means. They think the more countries join, the better it is for them, right? I can understand where they are coming from. A single country is weak, so it would be better to have more of them. But now that more and more countries are approaching them, even Muslim countries too, it is becoming increasingly unclear what NATO is. It's really complicated. It will get even more complicated next.

President Biden does not understand the significance of Ukraine

B
I think you are right in asking whether there is a reason for NATO to exist. In regard to the current case, it seems like the whole matter could have been resolved if the

U.S. had just said that NATO would not accept Ukraine as a member. Along these lines, is there a possibility of restoring peace?

PUTIN'S G.S.
The situation is a little different from yours. Europe lies right in front of them geopolitically from the American side, so it's like their front yard. And it looks more important to them. On the other hand, Japan and China are on the other side of Earth, so they can hardly see you. Geopolitically speaking, Europe is more important to them, and protecting Europe protects the U.S. This is how they see it. So, my guess is they can't be at ease until they get Russia to completely abandon its nuclear weapons.

Mr. Biden probably doesn't understand the significance of Ukraine or the significance of Crimea. He is simply saying that changing the territorial lines of the countries after World War II is not allowed. The U.S. has been at war over various things, but what was all that? What was the point of destroying Iraq, going to Afghanistan, getting involved in Vietnam, among other things? I do wonder what that was all about.

B

Then, considering Mr. Biden's level of understanding, you saw that it was impossible to negotiate and simply took action this time...

PUTIN'S G.S.

Frankly, his brain functions very slowly, like a snail.

B

Yes [*laughs wryly*]. So, I do sort of agree with you, but based on what you just said, it seems that you simply decided to ignore it for now and took action.

PUTIN'S G.S.

But it is actually about protecting the ethnic Russians. They are in trouble. They will be discriminated against in the future. They will be discriminated against because they are in another country. The same goes for Crimea. Seventy to eighty percent of them are ethnic Russians, but they are on the verge of being discriminated against and abused in the near future. I know that people on the other end are protesting and saying things like "Putin must die" because they fear for their own safety in case Russia invades, but this is a difficult issue. I am being forced to clean up Gorbachev's mess, though. Perhaps you want to make China be like Russia.

Revival of the Russian Empire is his dearest wish

A

Now that you have mentioned the Iraq War and the Vietnam War, I get the impression that President Putin may have some idea that is an antithesis to the order created by the U.S. after World War II or some kind of global vision. Do you have any thoughts on what the world should be like in the 21st century?

PUTIN'S G.S.

Although this may change in the future, at this point, the competing hegemonic powers are the U.S., Russia, China, and the EU. Perhaps the countries that are growing now could join in the future. They could be India or Brazil, but so far, they haven't reached that point yet. Right now, it's just the four of them. The U.S. might be thinking of making stronger ties with Latin America; however, if the U.S. doesn't know what Ukraine means to Russia, I think they should study what would happen to the U.S. if Latin America becomes a subsidiary of Russia.

A

In Europe, for example, President Macron of France is trying to mediate.

PUTIN'S G.S.

France is no good. Macron is incompetent. He shouldn't be marrying his schoolteacher. He is out of his mind. He is below average. I think his wife is making all the decisions. Well, more like his beloved former teacher. I think his beloved former teacher from high school or something is making all the policy decisions for the country. Such kinds of things are unacceptable. You have to be careful not to let unelected people control the government behind the scenes.

A

Right. Also, Germany, in reality, probably doesn't want to see this conflict escalate since they are actually quite dependent on Russia for energy. In fact, they have only sent helmets (to Ukraine). In this situation, I am wondering if you have any future plans for Russia in relation to Europe.

PUTIN'S G.S.

We have recovered a lot in the last 20 years, but you may not understand the sense of loss we are feeling. It is like the feeling you might have if Japan became smaller as a result of various parts of Japan being taken in addition to Okinawa, which the U.S. occupied for a few decades. And imagine them becoming independent. Now, the Russians who were losing confidence are getting a little more high-spirited. All the places Russia let go of are becoming conflict zones, which is not good. You could say that authority is bad, but in some ways, peace and order can be maintained thanks to a big authority. They have no idea what to do in the desert regions around Central Asia, Pakistan, Iran, Afghanistan, Iraq, Turkey, and Syria.

B

To summarize what you just said, restoring a part of Russian hegemony is a clear goal you have, among other objectives.

PUTIN'S G.S.

Yes, of course. The revival of the Russian Empire is among them. It is our dearest wish. I hope to get back as much of it as possible. I can't believe they were all dissolved at once. Gorbachev may have been popular, but our country was ruined because of him. It is as if Japan as a whole were broken up into separate prefectures. The Kanto region has 40 million people. So, it is like a country with a population of 120 million people shrinking to a country of 40 million people, and the rest of the regions becoming separated and independent. If the Allies had really been scared of Japan, they would have gone to that extent.

B
In that case, the next point of discussion will be about the current Russian system. For example, which is better, the political systems of Russia or those of western Europe? I mean, which political system is better for the citizens? The discussion about choosing a system will probably come up next. Are you confident about this as well?

PUTIN'S G.S.
So, looking at the current EU, it is basically an alliance of the weak. There are more countries that are simply hanging on to survive. They are the ones getting closer to socialism and creating "EU totalitarianism." It is as if a strange ghost called the EU has risen, and those who are trying to gain from it are attaching to it like leeches

sucking blood. There are a lot of countries that need to be cut off. A lot of countries are troublemakers, so they have to be cut off. So, that will be the next problem. The EU will turn into a hotbed of corruption.

His thoughts on Japan's position and China from now on

B

It sounds to me like you have a role to play in dismantling parts of the world that are lagging behind or are corrupt. Of course, I mean to say this in a good way. Does it mean you are actually conscious of this?

PUTIN'S G.S.

The times of the U.S., U.K., Germany, and France are over. It's done. Next, the time has come for Russia and Japan to decide on the world's movement. And we need to discuss how to deal with China. I don't think we should leave them as they are now. We will have to think about what to do with China. I don't think it's a bad idea to incorporate the Uyghur, Tibetan, and Mongolian Autonomous Regions into Russian territory.

B

That is a very possible choice...

PUTIN'S G.S.

They would be happier that way.

B

It may not be a bad idea for them to be an autonomous region within Russia or a democratic, highly autonomous country.

PUTIN'S G.S.

Then, Japan could be a little safer. I think it is dirty of them (China) to hold that area hostage. Since there are many nuclear missile sites in the Uyghur Autonomous Region, they will be targeted, right? Even though the Uyghurs are being oppressed, they will be the ones to get killed if a war starts. China is doing terrible things.

Even regarding pandas, they don't belong to China. They belong to Tibet. They should give them back to Tibet! Isn't that right? Pandas are Tibetan. These are the kinds of things that need to be corrected. Anyway, China and Russia are "bitter enemies in the same boat" and are still not on cordial terms.

However, you should be afraid of whether our activities in Ukraine will help China take Taiwan; you should fear the possibility of them making moves beyond Taiwan and trying to take the Philippines, Myanmar, Thailand, and Vietnam, or even invading India as well. With this in mind, it is not such a bad thing for Russia to be somewhat strong. If Russia is strong, China will be nervous. They are trying to extend their front to the south, but they can't do it if there is a threat to the north. I think it is better for Russia to be somewhat strong.

B

In this context, for example, if the current Ukraine conflict hadn't happened and China started to advance southward or invade Taiwan, would Russia help besiege China together with Japan and the West rather than backing China up? I understand this may be a difficult question now because there are various interests involved.

PUTIN'S G.S.

The EU is powerless now. Although the U.K. sent an aircraft carrier off the coast of Hong Kong, and Germany and Canada sent ships, they are not in any condition to fight. They shouldn't be so proud just because they sent a ship or two. If there is an actual war, they will lose badly. They don't have much power. They are just carrying out their PR activities. So, how we treat India is also becoming very important now. The Indian and Russian military actually have a very close relationship.

B
Yes, you're right.

PUTIN'S G.S.
Seventy percent of India's military technology and equipment is Russian-made. So, Russia and India are actually in a position to act together militarily. If Russia, Japan, and India can form a triangle, China's hegemony can be suppressed.

Why Putin's guardian spirit thinks the West is finished

B
So you are saying, in a way, if the U.S. initiative is weak, we have that option.

PUTIN'S G.S.

Isn't the whole continent of (North) America going to sink soon? Ask the space people. They are probably going to sink it. The U.S. has been doing a lot of bad things. After all the bad things they have done, it is about time they sank. I think Hollywood will sink to the bottom of the ocean—just like in your movie.

A

Looking at the world situation as a whole, the EU is no good because it is becoming quite leftist and socialist.

PUTIN'S G.S.

Yes, they are useless. They are all welfare states. They are all dependent. This is not the case for Russia now. We are doing our best on our own based on Master Okawa's teaching of self-help.

A

The Democratic Party administration in the U.S. is also significantly leaning toward the left.

PUTIN'S G.S.

You don't need the Democrats. They should be destroyed. The attack on the Capitol building was right, and all the Democrats should have been killed. [*While gesturing as if using a machine gun.*] Ba-ba-ba-ba. Then, the U.S. would have become stronger under a one-party dictatorship. Why did fake news like that come up? They should have killed everyone. Mr. Trump should have pushed it that far. Instead of saying, "Let's march to the Capitol," if he had given everyone a machine gun and said, "Go, go, go!" they could have killed everyone. You only need a couple of hundred people to do that. They should have done it before the National Guard showed up. Then, a one-party dictatorship of the Trump Party would have been formed.

A

While the West is wary of you, President Putin, in fact, your vision further includes an effective antithesis to the declining West, right?

PUTIN'S G.S.

Europe and America are already finished. They are outdated. Their ideas are too old. So, I'm thinking of elaborating on a new plan.

Also, I think it would be nice if nations like Russia, Japan, India, and Brazil became the world leaders of the next era. Indonesia seems to be developing, too. Their population has increased considerably. Europe and America have done pretty bad things in their 500-year history of colonization. They will be punished by God. I think they have to repent for their deeds, even just a little. They consider themselves superior races, so they should reflect on themselves.

Japan fought two wars against China and won both times. Japan defeated Russia, too. They only lost to the U.S., so Japan should be frustrated about that. If Russia and Japan fight together and defeat the U.S., then you've won against all countries. I don't think Russia would lose if it's a nuclear war. We have more nuclear weapons, so it's not that we can't do it. In fact, our weapons are now more advanced than the U.S. from a technical point of view.

Is God starting to choose which people to reduce?

PUTIN'S G.S.

How should we rebuild the world from now on? Well, God's voice says... Anyway, I have to do it. Hmm... But for now, I haven't heard the space beings saying to attack Russia, although I don't know if Master Okawa is supporting them. They do think China is dangerous, but they also think Biden is a problem. It seems that to them, Biden is a two-headed alien. For me, it seems like his head will split open in half.

A

In your mind, you consider yourself to be an agent of God, or someone who is close to Him and understands the intention of the heavenly world, and you have been taking various measures.

PUTIN'S G.S.

Now, the situation is progressing much more than you think. The world population is said to be eight billion now, but the God of the world has no intention of increasing it to 10 billion. Such a decision has been made.

Depending on the situation, the world population may be reduced to four billion or even to two billion, according to some (refer to "King Midas's Spiritual Message" recorded on February 9, 2022). For example, let's say the population will be reduced by four billion. So, the decision-making process on which population to reduce has already started. The question now is which population will be chosen. Therefore, a game of "musical chairs"—choosing which population to be reduced has begun.

B
Ah, I see.

PUTIN'S G.S.
In Russia, Japanese anime has become popular, and everyone is watching anime. It's just that you don't know about it. Many people have and sleep with body pillows that have pictures of female anime characters of Akihabara on it. The Japanese news media are wrong and don't know any better. So, I'd like them to understand the situation better.

8

Surprising Connections between Japan and Putin

What is the aim of Russia's "No evangelism outside of Church"?

C

Russia approved legislation that restricts missionary activities, so Happy Science has become unable to conduct its missionary work openly. We want to become more influential and spread Master's teachings more widely. But in reality, we are having difficulty distributing our books and conveying the teachings in Russia. The law prohibits missionary activities of religion. Was the passing of this legislation based on the true thoughts of President Putin? I would like to ask President Putin, who values the Will of God, what his thoughts are on bringing the light of God into the future of Russia?

PUTIN'S G.S.

There is a possibility for various thoughts to flow in from the West and shake Russia from the inside, so we have started to defend ourselves against such influences. The Russian Orthodox Church is supposed to be the state religion of Russia, but it feels a little strange to me that the Jewish god is enshrined in many churches in Russia. It (Israel) is too far from us.

Having said that, this has to do with why Russia is supporting the Syrian government forces. That area is actually where Jesus was spreading his teachings. I think Paul's Damascene conversion occurred on his way to Syria. So, in the future, this area will be... the battlefield of the one after the next war. Pakistan, Iran, Afghanistan, Iraq, and then the nations around Israel like Saudi Arabia... These Islamic nations don't get along with each other, so there is a possibility for the next war to start in these areas, too. But I don't know if a hegemony will emerge.

I think Biden intends to attack Iran in a time of need. But I don't think the U.S. has the capability to do it. There is a possibility of the U.S. declining if it takes clumsy measures.

From the Russian perspective, Japan appears to be a quasi-colony of the U.S.

PUTIN'S G.S.

It might have been OK for Japan to fawn on the U.S. for a short while after World War II when the U.S. occupied it, but Japan has to stop it now. I think Japan made a mistake after the war; Japan had to amend the constitution when Douglas MacArthur said it was OK for Japan to do so at the time of the Korean War. Japanese politicians who didn't amend the constitution then were useless. They were really useless. The other politicians who couldn't do anything after that were useless, too. Japan had to amend its constitution when MacArthur said Japan should be armed after the occupation of Japan. After all, I do think it's a problem that Japan couldn't change its constitution for decades and left it unrevised.

While I, myself, think so, I don't know how you feel about it. You may think you are living in a free and peaceful nation, but from our viewpoint, Japan is still a quasi-colony of the U.S. It appears that way to us. So, I want Japan to be Japan. It's about time Japan freed itself from being America's colony. If the U.S. hears what I'm saying, they would probably say that Russia has started a conspiracy to shake the Japan-U.S. alliance.

Unfortunately, the Japanese political leaders are not independent-minded enough when they should be. That is why they don't think much of China's claim that Okinawa is China's core interest; they didn't care when South Korea claimed that Takeshima belonged to them nor when China claimed that the Senkaku Islands belonged to them. The Japanese political leaders conclude the issues by saying, "It's deplorable," or "We strongly object." I think Japan is in danger. I think it's in serious danger.

Japan doesn't exist on Biden's world map. You have to understand this well. The number of Happy Science members in Russia is about 100 or 200 at best, right? That is nothing. It's such a small number. It will spread with a bang when it spreads. So, don't worry. You need to come in from the political side.

Even Aum Shinrikyo, which is almost extinct in Japan, had 30,000 members (in Russia) for a while. They were far more advanced than you in this regard. I think your power to spread your teachings is quite weak, but I also think parts of your teachings are not understood easily because you are dealing with such diverse values.

So, the next problem should be how to deal with Russia and the Islamic nations. But I don't think the U.S. has any solutions regarding this. A nation like Russia is vast from the east to the west. Russia cannot be treated so lightly in the same way they treat American democracy, where candidates were asking people to vote using a stagecoach. No way. That's beyond impossible. Well... Does it seem like I'm just trying to draw you closer to us?

A
No, no, you've already given us five or six spiritual messages. I believe you're placing your hopes on us.

PUTIN'S G.S.
Well, I thought we were already friends...

A
Yes. And in a way, you care more about and are more concerned for Japan than the Japanese politicians.

PUTIN'S G.S.
That's right.

Why Putin's guardian spirit is strongly interested in getting closer to Japan

A

One thing I want to ask you is that last September (2021), Mr. Putin's guardian spirit came calling himself Ivan IV (see Extra Chapter). Is it Ivan IV who is here today?

PUTIN'S G.S.

You listed up some really great figures as my past lives.

A

Yes.

PUTIN'S G.S.

Augustus[2], Emperor Shomu[3], Ashikaga Yoshimasa[4], Ivan IV, Tokugawa Yoshimune[5], and Putin. Wow. I'll be a god next [*laughs*], at this rate.

A

[*Laughs.*] If you are Ivan IV, then you must be envisioning reviving Russia and making it a great power again. Is there also a spiritual connection between Russia and Japan that we don't know about?

PUTIN'S G.S.

Looking at the past lives, three of them are Japanese, right? Of them, the part of me that is Emperor Shomu is strongly interested in approaching Japan now. I feel Japan is trying to go back to the time when the Great Buddha statue was built. Should the U.S. or Europe attack us and I have to defect, I would defect to Japan, so please take care of me.

A

I really believe you have the caliber to be the president in Japan.

PUTIN'S G.S.

No, no, I do not have that much power. But it is sad that there is a sense of distance between us and Japan. Do we need the Korean Peninsula? They're in the way, aren't they? North Korea and South Korea are obstructing our relations. Maybe they should stop using Hangul. I would give the peninsula to Japan. They should have stayed a part of Japan. They had been under Japan's colonial rule for 35 years anyway. Then Japan and Russia could be connected. Perfect. Will they be mad at me for saying this?

A

Well, hmm...

PUTIN'S G.S.

Hmm. Are there many (Happy Science) members in South Korea?

A

The Russo-Japanese War was fought over the Korean Peninsula, so Japan will be glad to know that President Putin feels this way.

PUTIN'S G.S.

North Korea can't be trusted, but South Korea is a terrible country, too. It cannot in any way be called a proper nation. It's not a developed country at all.

And in their current presidential election, a candidate is saying he will make South Korea a part of the five great powers? Oh, please. They can't think for themselves. The country is like a crawling octopus. We don't need a country like that. We don't need anything other than their barbeque culture. Don't you think so?

A

Let me confirm this. Are you Ivan IV himself?

PUTIN'S G.S.

Well, no...

A

Or Emperor Shomu?

PUTIN'S G.S.

All the guardian spirits are here. It's a combined entity. We are all here when we give our opinion, from Shomu to Yoshimune.

Japan should be stronger and spread Japanese values

A

Japan and Russia must come up with a vision for the world of the 21st century...

PUTIN'S G.S.

You have to have ambitions. If you don't, you'll remain a colony. In fact, you are a de facto quasi-colony of the United States. Japan defeated the Russian Empire, right? And you beat China twice, right? The Chinese people think they'll lose again if Japan gets serious. They know they are weak, although they have a larger population. They think Japan could crush China if it really wanted to. Didn't Japan take over mainland China in just a few months? Really. That's how strong you are.

You already had an aircraft carrier fleet 80 years ago. Japan is powerful if you let yourselves be. But you have tied up your own hands and feet. Maybe a little crisis could shake things up.

I think Japan should be stronger. In a sense, the world is looking to the Japanese way of thinking. It's not as violent as the U.S. It doesn't have ethnocentric views like the Sinocentrism which China has. Also, it's not a veiled gang of burglars like the Islamic world. I think Japanese values should spread throughout the world more.

We don't need Islam anymore, no? Islam can stop being a world religion now. That's how I feel. A new idea should be created while inheriting the values of Buddhism and Christianity. Islam is always starting wars. It's a source of conflict. It's very similar to Mao Zedong's military-first policies. It's not a very good religion. You (Happy Science) seem to defend them, but I think it's time to abandon them. I think the time has come for that.

However, I believe Muslim countries look up to Japan. Islam is also spreading in African countries, but I think it would be better if the Islamic world believed in the Japanese religion.

9

The Prospect of the World According to Putin's Guardian Spirit

China should take responsibility for spreading coronavirus around the world

A

Today, we saw that you are thinking about the world situation from a global perspective. We also saw that you have high expectations for Japan.

PUTIN'S G.S.

We have about 200,000 troops deployed (around Ukraine). The U.S. is saying that it will send 3,000 or 5,000, but that will be nothing. Biden is pretending to take action by just doing things like imposing economic sanctions or sending some troops to Poland.

If needed, we'll shoot missiles at them, really. I'll do it until that old man is scared out of his pants. I'll do that much. I'm a "dictator." But the nice thing about dictators is that they get the job done, like Mr. Trump. Even North

Korea was held down when Mr. Trump was president. If he were the president right now, North Korea would not be launching missiles. It would have talked with Mr. Trump and tried to change the country into a country like Vietnam and make it develop economically.

Americans made the wrong choice in that rigged election. I think it needs to be undone. Biden received bribes... or at least his son received bribes through his company. Keeping such a person as president will lead to poor judgment regarding China and Russia.

Over 400 million people are infected (with coronavirus) globally. The number will probably go up to more than one billion and the death toll to the tens of millions. China should take responsibility for this. The course of action that the world should take is to prevent Russia and China from joining hands.

How to deter China's military threats

PUTIN'S G.S.
The U.S. and NATO working together to impose sanctions on Russia will only cause the world to be divided. It is

wrong. Please leave Ukraine to Russia. We'll look after it. The U.S. does not need to interfere. It's none of their business, honestly. Frankly, the U.S. should just stick to tending cattle in Texas.

If it is such a great country, people in Central or South America will use English, don't you think? They should be using English at work. But they don't. They hate America. Americans are very egoistic. You will know it once you get close to them.

So, I don't wish for the world to be painted entirely in the U.S. color, but I welcome Japan to become a more powerful country, and I would like to get along with you a little better. Russia and Japan allied together will be able to deter China's military threats.

The U.S. is starting to fight with Russia, but it'll end up embarrassing itself soon. Actually, no, it has already embarrassed itself in Afghanistan. The U.S. failed in the Iraq War, too, right? Claiming that Iraq had weapons of mass destruction, it went to war, occupied Iraq, and hanged the president, but it turned out that Iraq had no such weapons.

The U.S. should really apologize to the world. It is an aggressor nation. It should apologize, but instead, it acts as nothing happened. This hegemony shouldn't be allowed to have its own way. It makes mistakes. Half of what the U.S. does is absolutely wrong. In my opinion, it should choose the right half and reduce the wrong half.

Biden says Putin has no right to officially recognize the two regions as independent states. But they used to be part of our country, and Russians live there, and they're asking for protection. As a leader, I have to do something about it. Russian people over there could be subjected to genocide. I have to do something to help them. It's a matter of course. The EU countries would never help them. I bet the people would end up like the Muslim refugees. They would be discriminated against, struggle to get jobs and be poor.

It's true that we were able to win the wars against Napoleon and Hitler because of the Ukrainian region. Master Okawa seems to know this very well. If it had not been for Ukraine, there is a very good chance that we would have lost both wars. So, this region is more important to our defense against Europe than you'd think. That's why I cannot compromise on this, so there is no other choice.

If someone said, "You don't need Okinawa or Kyushu" or "Let's give Hokkaido to the Soviet Union or Russia,"

I'm sure you won't accept that. Should Russia march south into Hokkaido and claim its independence saying, "Japan took this land from the Ainu people. Japan is evil. This is now the Republic of Ainu," then, of course, you might be angry, but that is not the case for Ukraine. Speaking of which, what about the Native American territories in the U.S.? They took other people's land too, didn't they? But the question is whether the people are better off or not.

So, if you (Interviewer C) can't spread the teachings of Happy Science, it's because you're doing missionary activities like it's a business. You have to do it on a much larger scale. The first step is for you to join the Japanese administration. Or rather, your political party has to be able to give opinions as representatives of the nation. Then there will be things you can do more openly.

I brought back the Russian Orthodox Church for now; it's better than atheism. It's better than atheism or materialism. Russian people believe in God, and they're religious, and I also pray. So, if God's idea is to move on to the next stage, I think I have to support and protect that indirectly to some extent, and that is the fundamental difference between us and China.

Putin's guardian spirit encourages Japan to be neutral

A
Thank you very much for sharing your valuable thoughts with us today.

PUTIN'S G.S.
We have to be careful because Biden could continue going out of control. I would at least like Japan to... Japan is talking about financial sanctions against Russia in step with other countries, but there may not be any benefit to doing so. It may be better for Japan to stay neutral. Think about it. I guess Prime Minister Kishida won't be thinking about it. It's a pity that Mr. Abe got so close to concluding the peace treaty but couldn't follow through in the end. He didn't have enough courage, I guess. The Russian ambassador in Japan seemed to feel truly sad about being notified of Japan's sanctions against Russia. I guess the ambassador must have wanted Japan to get along with Russia. I pray that more powerful leaders will emerge in Japan.

In terms of your complaints about missionary activities, I think there is a need for you to gain a little more political power. Otherwise, it will continue to look like Master Okawa's opinion is the only one with influence, and the rest of you are just there to collect your salaries. In any case, you need to have proper power. To be honest, his disciples are probably not very popular. That's what I think. So, you need to become more popular. Japan has constantly been subjected to brainwashing, so it's also your job to reverse its effects.

Russia internally feels a certain degree of affinity to Happy Science. But, actually, I'm making laws and such to prohibit speaking ill of the people like the first and second founding leaders of the former Soviet Union, so you might be feeling it's difficult to criticize them. But things should be OK as long as you say Putin is someone close to God or is a god himself.

One thing he would like to say about the virus

A

I think today's talk has considerably mitigated the biases of the views of Western society. It has also shown us, Japanese people, your honest expectations for Japan very clearly.

PUTIN'S G.S.

You will soon start to feel like something needs to be done about the pointless gathering of 20 or 30 countries. I'm tempted to say to Hitler of Germany, "Be reborn clean and lead the people." Then, negotiation with them (EU) would be possible. In the current situation, I can't even tell whom I should negotiate with.

A

After listening to your message, in a way, I thought the Middle East and Europe could be stabilized if President Putin's vision is mostly realized.

PUTIN'S G.S.

Also, the U.K. left the EU. Prime Minister Boris Johnson is saying that the omicron strain is just like the flu and that they will cancel all preventative measures to resume their normal lives. I think this approach would be OK against omicron, but China has the next viral weapon ready—this weapon is more powerful and has an extremely high fatality rate. I just want to tell him not to lower his guard because it would be a pity if the U.K. vanished from the earth.

In the end... The coronavirus also killed many Russian people. At least hundreds of thousands of them died from it. I will make China pay the price for what they have done.

Can President Putin hear the voice of God?

A

Today, we received opinions from a standpoint closer to God...

PUTIN'S G.S.

Well, Mr. Trump could hear God's voice too, but Biden can't, right? I can hear God's voice. It's no use supporting those who can't hear it. For now, Russia and China are "bitter enemies in the same boat," but at present, Russia has no direct relationship with the evil space people to which China is connected. I'm telling you, Russia is different from them.

A

Yes. Thank you very much for your valuable message today.

PUTIN'S G.S.

Wouldn't it be better for Japan to annex the Korean Peninsula and even Taiwan? You shouldn't just stop at Okinawa and should just annex all of them, including the southern part of China, to the "Japan Union." Imagine if Japan had ruled China! China would have been happy by now. I really feel sorry for that country. The U.S. did some unnecessary things. Don't you think so? I think they did.

A

Yes. I also understood very well that you have a solid opinion about the post-war system in Japan.

PUTIN'S G.S.

I said what I wanted to say. It's just that the leaders are weak in Japan. You have to work on that. My term of office and Master Okawa's "term of office" may overlap. I will also do my job. I'll make it to the end. So, you can still trust me. I'm not finished yet.

A

I look forward to it. Thank you very much.

10

You Cannot Rely Only on Information from the West to Understand the Situation in Ukraine

RYUHO OKAWA

[*Claps twice.*] Well, he seems to be doing pretty well, but I don't know about the people around him. But it's actually true that there are many things he can do at his discretion. Mr. Trump had a similar tendency. Mr. Putin appeared around the time when the Soviet Union collapsed and the country of Russia was about to disappear. What enables Putin to do these things is the fact that he rebuilt Russia in 20 years. Of course, I'm sure he is taking the sanctions into account as he does what he does.

I agree with his opinion that Mr. Trump would have done the same thing as what Mr. Putin did. I'm sure Mr. Trump would have done the same thing. Unless that region (Ukraine) is secured, Russia will be in danger in the future. There is a risk of their country disappearing. There is a possibility that only the Siberian region will be left for Russia, so I can understand his perspective to some extent. However, I hope he will address it as peacefully as possible.

I doubt anyone in the Japanese media will say anything like this. Perhaps it would have been better if more progress had been made when Mr. Abe was in office. I hope Mr. Biden won't dig his own grave. The two-party system is fine, but I think it is a problem if the U.S. foreign policy changes every time the party changes.

This time, Mr. Biden seems to be trying to prevent Mr. Trump's revival by denouncing the Russian connection. I'm a little concerned he may be mixing up private and public matters. So, I think we cannot rely only on information from the West.

It's difficult. Iran is also facing difficulties because of the sanctions imposed on them. So, they have to make ties with China. That's why it is getting harder for us to become friends with Iran. Now, the question is how to get along with this difficult Muslim country and other countries. It's going to be a difficult task.

Unfortunately, having less than one percent of the Japanese people's support is not enough to change the country. It would be good if we could do the same thing that

Choshu and Satsuma[6] Domains did to change the Tokugawa regime. Just like they were able to change the regime with their level of influence, we, Happy Science, should also be able to turn Japan around with our current strength. Well, I think education and the mass media play a big role. There is nothing that can be done about it right away.

Russia will draw a barrage of criticisms, but in any case, we heard his opinion, and we will present this to the world. I think it will probably overlap with about 80 percent of what Mr. Putin himself would say.

Many people say that Russia's military activities will encourage China to take military action. If that's how people see the situation, I must make myself clear that we, Happy Science, do not agree with China's military action.

After all, we must pursue those who are responsible for the coronavirus pandemic. I think the UN will soon give up regarding China. This means the UN itself is no longer functioning. It's on its way to collapse. Therefore, we need to think about how we will create the next international order or the next 100-year plan.

We may soon see missiles being fired or tanks rolling in. We don't know what will happen. We may face headwinds for what we are saying and draw criticisms.

However, this is the way we do things at Happy Science, so we will express our opinions as they are.

I don't think Putin is under the control of the devil, at least for now. I think he has remained unchanged, so I want to take this into consideration as we address this issue. Well, today was just about presenting his opinions.

A
Thank you very much for today.

TRANSLATOR'S NOTES

1 Namamugi Incident

An incident that occurred during the late Edo period in 1862 when 4 British horsemen interrupted the procession of which the father of Satsuma Domain's leader was returning home. As a result, one horseman was killed, and two others were injured. This incident triggered the Anglo-Satsuma war in the following year.

2 Augustus (Octavius) (63 B.C. - 14 A.D.)

The first emperor of the Roman Empire. He took after Julius Caesar and worked to bring an end to internal conflicts and establish peace. Augustus unified the Mediterranean world and created the Roman Empire, establishing Pax Romana (Roman peace).

3 Emperor Shomu (701 - 756)

An emperor during the Nara period. He was a devout Buddhist and conducted Buddhist policies together with Empress Komyo in order to appease and protect the nation. Emperor Shomu built provincial temples across Japan for monks (kokubun-ji) and nuns (kokubun-niji). Also, he built Todai-ji which upholds the Great Buddha as the object of faith (honzon), by having Gyoki be the one actually responsible for it.

4 Yoshimasa Ashikaga (1436 - 1490)

The 8th shogun of the Muromachi Shogunate. He left the operations of the shogunate administration up to people such as Tomiko Hino, his official wife, and Sozen Yamana, a powerful guardian daimyo. Yoshimasa himself put to use his exceptional leadership and eye in the artistic aspect, such as in developing the Higashiyama culture. He also built Ginkakuji, which is the building modeled after Kinkakuji that his grandfather, Yoshimitsu, had built.

5 Yoshimune Tokugawa (1684 - 1751)

The 8th shogun of the Edo Shogunate. He conducted the Kyoho Reforms to reconstruct the financial status of the shogunate from bankruptcy. He was one of the best political leaders during the Edo period.

6 Choshu and Satsuma

Choshu and Satsuma were domains of West Japan in the Edo period. Although they were far from the capital, they later became the central power of the movement to overthrow the Edo Shogunate, lead the Meiji Restoration (1868), and modernize Japan.

These spiritual messages were channeled through Ryuho Okawa. However, please note that because of his high level of enlightenment, his way of receiving spiritual messages is fundamentally different from other psychic mediums who undergo trances and are completely taken over by the spirits they are channeling. When Master Okawa channels spirits who do not speak Japanese, they are sometimes able to use vocabulary from his language center to communicate their spiritual messages in Japanese.

It should be noted that these spiritual messages are opinions of the individual spirits and may contradict the ideas or teachings of Happy Science Group.

EXTRA CHAPTER

Spiritual Message from Ivan IV, the First Tsar of Russia

Ivan IV Talks about Russia's Struggle and the Drifting World

Originally recorded in Japanese on September 14, 2021
at the Special Lecture Hall of Happy Science in Japan
and later translated into English.

Ivan IV (1530-1584)

The grandson of Ivan III. He became the grand prince of Moscow at age three and declared himself Tsar of all Russia at age 16. He conquered Kazan and Astrakhan and started to intrude into even Siberia. He established commercial ties with England. On the other hand, he lost the Crimean raids and the Livonian War, which thwarted his advance into the Black Sea and the Baltic Sea.

Domestically, he restricted the mobility of the peasants, strengthening the system of serfdom. Despite being called a brutal ruler, he possessed extraordinary political abilities and greatly contributed to the development of Russia's culture and commerce. He is known as "Ivan the Terrible" for having ruled the aristocrats by fear.

Interviewer from Happy Science*

Shio Okawa
  Aide to Master & CEO

---
* The title is at the time of the interview.

1
Ivan IV Appears, Fearing for the Future of Russia

The spirit of the Russian Tsar suddenly appeared in the middle of the night

SHIO OKAWA
Is someone here?

IVAN IV
[*After about five seconds of silence.*] It's pointless, I'm afraid.

SHIO OKAWA
What's pointless? Your talk?

IVAN IV
Yes. I'm Tsar Ivan IV.

SHIO OKAWA
I'm sorry?

Spiritual Message from Ivan IV, the First Tsar of Russia

IVAN IV
I said I'm Tsar Ivan IV.

SHIO OKAWA
Of Russia?

IVAN IV
Tsar of all Russia.

SHIO OKAWA
You are?

IVAN IV
Yes.

SHIO OKAWA
Why did you come now?

IVAN IV
That's why I'm saying it's pointless.

SHIO OKAWA
Well, I don't necessarily think so.

IVAN IV

I knew it was of no use, but I came here anyway.

SHIO OKAWA

Are you concerned about the future of Russia?

IVAN IV

I know this (spiritual message) won't be made public if I come in the middle of the night.

SHIO OKAWA

Well, if you speak well, it will be shown to people.

IVAN IV

But you don't know anything about me.

SHIO OKAWA

At least I know you're from Russia. I didn't imagine you could speak Japanese.

IVAN IV

Yes, I can.

SHIO OKAWA
You were made into movies.

IVAN IV
Oh right. They made some.

Views on Russia's move to approach China

SHIO OKAWA
What did you come to talk about today?

IVAN IV
Well, I'll tell you what, I'm born as Putin.

SHIO OKAWA
Wow! Is that right?

IVAN IV
Yes.

SHIO OKAWA
Are you saying that Mr. Putin was once born as Tsar Ivan IV in his past life?

IVAN IV

Yes.

SHIO OKAWA

Really?

IVAN IV

Yes.

SHIO OKAWA

I see.

IVAN IV

As Putin, I'm in trouble right now, you know. I had been negotiating (spiritually) with Happy Science, but it came to a deadlock.

SHIO OKAWA

Oh, are you saying that now you have no choice but to approach China?

IVAN IV

Yes, now I have to team up with China.

Spiritual Message from Ivan IV, the First Tsar of Russia

SHIO OKAWA
So that's why...

IVAN IV
While I'm concerned about North Korea's missiles, Russia has also built military bases on the Four Northern Islands to counter the U.S. and Japan. So I'm wondering if Russia appears to be the same as North Korea now.

SHIO OKAWA
I think Mr. Biden is largely responsible for that.

IVAN IV
He bullies Russia. He believes he can prevent Trump's comeback by bullying Russia.

SHIO OKAWA
That's right. Master Ryuho Okawa said that the world is divided and split into two because of Mr. Biden's lack of awareness.

IVAN IV
Well, I guess that's what's happening.

SHIO OKAWA

Yes, Master said that it's Mr. Biden—not Mr. Trump, who is leading the world into chaos and division.

IVAN IV

As Master Okawa predicted...

SHIO OKAWA

It became just as he said.

IVAN IV

Countries like North Korea, Russia, China, Pakistan, Afghanistan, and Iran are starting to connect with each other. Myanmar and other war-torn countries are going to be quite tough. If the U.S. draws a line, saying that they will not accept anything other than parliamentary democracy, then I don't see any strategy in it at all.

I wonder what he will do. I doubt Mr. Biden can say anything about North Korea's missiles that fly 1,500 kilometers (about 1,000 miles).

SHIO OKAWA

I wonder what he will say. I guess he will just make some comments in a Japanese way.

IVAN IV

By "a Japanese way," do you mean he will just suggest that they hold a talk sometime in the future?

SHIO OKAWA

I mean, he may say things like, "We will not tolerate North Korea's outrageous actions," only in words, and in reality, he will probably end up inviting a situation like Afghanistan.

IVAN IV

Well, Japan is expecting an election that will decide the next prime minister, so it is off guard now. Both North Korea and China see this as a chance. Japan will be in trouble if they plot something at a time like this.

But well... there's nothing you can do. I pity poor Japanese people.

SHIO OKAWA

I guess we have no choice but to get what we deserve...

IVAN IV

No other country is as far from the universal values.

SHIO OKAWA

Indeed. Japan has a unique value.

IVAN IV

The Meiji Restoration hasn't occurred yet in the truest sense.

I'm now (reborn) in Russia, so I'm going to rebuild Russia. But since it's been a long time (Putin being the president), other heads of state are beginning to get jealous of me. This makes things really difficult.

I suppose he will next be saying things like, "We must prepare for Putin's cyber-attack" or "There is a suspicion of bribery." He'll probably say that kind of stuff.

SHIO OKAWA

Do you mean Mr. Biden? Seriously, he is completely misreading the times.

IVAN IV

Well, but it's the media who supported such a man.

SHIO OKAWA

That's right. The U.S. is also in turmoil right now.

IVAN IV

That's why China is making moves as they like, and so is North Korea. Well, I'm afraid you might say Russia is going off as well.

SHIO OKAWA

There is gossip saying Kim Jong-un's face has changed or he lost weight. There could be secrets behind it. He wears a suit with a tie and...

IVAN IV

There's no problem wearing it since he owns some.

SHIO OKAWA

Well, that's true [*laughs*].

IVAN IV

He can't hide his belly in what he used to wear, but he can hide it in a fine suit. Maybe it wasn't a bad idea that he changed his hairstyle, though.

The difference in the approach to Russia between Trump and Biden

SHIO OKAWA
I'm afraid you are called "Ivan the Terrible."

IVAN IV
Yes, I suppose.

I'm in trouble because by now, some people want to oust me (President Putin) but I don't want to let Russia be America's enemy nation that supports the outlaws such as the Taliban and ISIS.

SHIO OKAWA
So it wasn't your intention.

IVAN IV
No, I don't want Russia to be like that. To be honest, as Master Okawa said, I was hoping for Russia to be included in the Western Bloc. But there is nothing I could...

SHIO OKAWA
So Mr. Biden's strategy is hugely responsible for that. Mr. Trump was trying to expand G7 (an intergovernmental

organization of the world's largest developed economies) to form G8, including Russia.

IVAN IV
Well...

SHIO OKAWA
I think he (Mr. Trump) probably thought Russia was more trustworthy than China.

IVAN IV
I think China is now in the midst of deciding on allies and foes.

SHIO OKAWA
It's possible that China is plotting something behind the scenes in Afghanistan. They are supporting them.

IVAN IV
Of course, that's obvious. China is backing the Taliban. They are also backing Myanmar.

Unfortunately, Russia won't benefit unless the opinions opposing the West are more or less accepted in the United Nations.

I guess Japan is also in turmoil. I don't think any of the candidates for the prime minister will do well (as of September 2021).

SHIO OKAWA

Since the start of the coronavirus pandemic, Master Ryuho Okawa has made various future predictions about politics as well. Things have been going as he predicted, so unless people realize the limitations of their current ways of thinking, I don't think things will get any better.

IVAN IV

Ah [*sighs*]. People just use global warming to explain why things aren't going well in the world. They're helpless. You

What Will Become of Coronavirus Pandemic? (Tokyo: HS Press, 2020)

Shakyamuni Buddha's Future Prediction (Tokyo: HS Press, 2020)

know, the current politicians think they won't be around by the target year they are discussing.

What to do with Russia... It's difficult for Russia.

SHIO OKAWA

Yes, it is. Is it not possible for Russia to express its will in a way that the U.S. can better understand it?

IVAN IV

What will?

SHIO OKAWA

For example, the will to accept Western-style values to some extent.

IVAN IV

We have actually adopted such values to a large extent compared to the past.

SHIO OKAWA

I think in Mr. Biden's mind, Russia is still the same as the former Soviet Union.

IVAN IV

Hmm... Well, he might set us up as a potential enemy at any time. Certainly, if Russia and China join hands, the U.S. cannot take any action, and if we line up Pakistan, Afghanistan, and Iran, we can contain India and Israel.

SHIO OKAWA

Is China giving such offers?

IVAN IV

China is planning to build the One Belt One Road, so of course, they must be thinking of conquering them.

SHIO OKAWA

That's true.

Spiritual Message from Ivan IV, the First Tsar of Russia

2

Concerns about the Current Situation in Japan

Wondering what Russia can do against China

IVAN IV

You must be at a loss because the world is going away from what you have been aiming for in this global turmoil. Happy Science is actually the religion that must arise at a time of national crisis like this, and the same is true for your political party (Happiness Realization Party), but it's a pity that you can't do anything.

SHIO OKAWA

One reason is that the Earth's population has grown large, and many people have different ways of thinking. I guess it is partly due to the weaknesses of democracy as well.

IVAN IV

[*Five seconds of silence.*] Hmm...

SHIO OKAWA

I don't think it's just the matter of whether we (Happiness Realization Party) will run (for the election) or not. I think it's the time when humanity needs to awaken.

IVAN IV

You were trying to thaw the diplomatic relations with Russia and Iran, but your efforts might have been brought to naught at the moment.

(Taro) Kono may say something eccentric, but I don't think any global issues will ultimately be solved with his leadership. (Sanae) Takaichi won't understand world affairs either because her ideas are based on a local perspective.[1] She won't be able to conduct diplomacy with a bird's-eye view of the world. (Fumio) Kishida will just end up being a typical Japanese political leader. That's the impression I've got.

SHIO OKAWA

Well... Since the Japanese people are fine with them, it can't be helped. Unless people realize something, we have no other choice.

IVAN IV

As Ivan IV, I am focused on making Russia strong. I want to make it even stronger. Well, I don't know how far we can go with China, though.

I'm afraid I might have failed Master Ryuho Okawa.

SHIO OKAWA

It is fine for you to make Russia strong, but we want you to do so in accordance with God's justice. If you end up supporting the spread of China's ways of thinking throughout the world, then the future of Russia will also be dark.

IVAN IV

Well, I wonder if there is anything else I can do.

Japan forced itself to hold the Olympics, but it only led to the resignation of Mr. Suga (Japanese prime minister, 2020 - 2021). That was the only effect.

Well... With the way it is now, I guess Greta Thunberg will end up being the savior of the world.

SHIO OKAWA

If that happens, humanity will have to face some hardship as a counteraction. If people don't realize their mistakes, we'll just have to accept the hardship.

IVAN IV

Hmm... What to do with Mongolia, the Uyghur region, Tibet, Hong Kong, and Taiwan? In terms of Russia's position, as the way things are now, we basically can't do anything for them. We can't make any moves because we've also been accused that Russia invaded Crimea and criticized in the same way as China is criticized.

SHIO OKAWA

Yes, Russia is regarded as the same (as China) by the human rights advocates within the U.S. Democratic Party.

IVAN IV

I'm sure that's how they see us. If that's the case, then it's likely that we are seen as the same as the terrorists who attacked the World Trade Center.

SHIO OKAWA

Even a well-known professor at the University of Tokyo in Japan criticized Mr. Trump—not China, referring to Hannah Arendt. It seems even political scientists can no longer correctly see who is on the side of genocide, dictatorship, or totalitarianism.

IVAN IV

Hmm, I understand Japan is going through tough battles in every respect.

SHIO OKAWA

In a way, it's really Mr. Biden who is self-centered. He only thinks about America, not in the sense of Mr. Trump's "America First" policy. The guardian spirit of Mr. Biden said that Japan would be a battlefield, and he may be right on this point (refer to *Spiritual Interviews with the Guardian Spirits of Biden and Trump*).

IVAN IV

I myself have thought like that, so I knew it would... Now we're heading toward the worst-case scenario.

SHIO OKAWA

The other day, Mr. Yaidron also said things are moving in the worst-case scenario (refer to *Spiritual Messages from Yaidron: Save the World from Destruction*).

IVAN IV

The fact that North Korea has 1,500-kilometer range cruise missiles means that they can attack Japan, but not the U.S. mainland, right?

SHIO OKAWA

That's right.

IVAN IV

They can attack South Korea and Japan. There is no point in firing at China and Russia because North Korea cannot withstand their retaliation.

Spiritual Interviews with the Guardian Spirits of Biden and Trump (Tokyo: HS Press, 2020)

Spiritual Messages from Yaidron: Save the World from Destruction (Tokyo: HS Press, 2021)

Spiritual Message from Ivan IV, the First Tsar of Russia

About the mission to make Russia strong

SHIO OKAWA
Why did you come here, now, as Tsar Ivan IV?

IVAN IV
Huh? Because I have this mission to make Russia strong.

SHIO OKAWA
I see. So you had actually returned to heaven...

IVAN IV
Well, I did become a movie.

SHIO OKAWA
Yes, indeed.

IVAN IV
There aren't many heroes in Russia. It's a pity that your books of spiritual messages didn't have much effect. I (Putin), too, issued a law banning people from speaking badly of Lenin or Stalin. That's because those people will become the same force that criticizes me. They will criticize the dictatorship and the dictator.

SHIO OKAWA

Nowadays, in democratic countries as a whole, people fail to identify the real dictator and instead mistake those showing strong leadership in a good way for dictators.

IVAN IV

Hmm.

SHIO OKAWA

Mr. Trump and Mr. Putin are seen as dictators, but no one can really criticize the real dictators. Although everyone knows that Mr. Xi Jinping and Mr. Kim Jong-un are dictators (they cannot stop them and) those with strong leadership are treated as such dictators of the same level.

IVAN IV

I don't want the age to come when Kim Jong-un can threaten South Korea and Japan. But I myself wish for Russia to develop. I wonder who will settle all this.

Spiritual Message from Ivan IV, the First Tsar of Russia

Concerns about the situation Japan might have to face

SHIO OKAWA
Ever since the coronavirus pandemic started, we have asked various spirits and space beings for their opinions. They say that the world might become completely darkened.

IVAN IV
But you won't be able to fulfill your mission by just listening to what they have to say. It's true that something unusual often happens with climate, though.

SHIO OKAWA
It must be partly because of a divine will, but all the blame is put on global warming now. People believe that science is almighty. Even facing the coronavirus pandemic, they believe only in medicine and say it's stupid to pray to God.

IVAN IV
I wonder what they really want.

Certainly, looking at the issues of North Korea's missiles, China's missiles and aircraft carriers, and our building of the military bases in the Northern Territories, Japan cannot let its guard down from now on.

SHIO OKAWA
But I'm afraid only very few people in Japan think they must be on guard.

IVAN IV
Hmm.

SHIO OKAWA
Japanese people probably have entirely different recognition from those in the rest of the world.

IVAN IV
We have different issues with Ukraine, but we're thought to be similar to Syria, where the government orders the use of poison gas weapons.

Ah, the Happiness Realization Party... I wonder why it was not so popular.

Spiritual Message from Ivan IV, the First Tsar of Russia

SHIO OKAWA

Regardless of the Happiness Realization Party, the U.S. makes independent moves. I think the current scenario was inevitable the moment the U.S. chose Mr. Biden.

3

Views on President Biden and the Coronavirus Pandemic

Master Okawa's remark that gave hope to Ivan IV

IVAN IV

It's going to be chaotic. I think the world will be in chaos.

SHIO OKAWA

Yes, the world will be in chaos. I'm sure God knows Mr. Putin is also in trouble.

IVAN IV

I'm actually in trouble because Russia cannot find a way out.

SHIO OKAWA

Right. Are there any other Russian gods?

IVAN IV

Well, I am like the god of Russia.

Spiritual Message from Ivan IV, the First Tsar of Russia

SHIO OKAWA

That's what I thought.

IVAN IV

That's how it is.

SHIO OKAWA

Doesn't God Odin visit you?

IVAN IV

I used to receive his guidance in the past.

SHIO OKAWA

You now come to our Master for advice, I suppose.

IVAN IV

I don't think Russia is making moves in favor of Japan. It is a pity we couldn't benefit from Mr. Abe's only strength.

SHIO OKAWA

That's right. Mr. Putin even came all the way to Yamaguchi Prefecture.

IVAN IV

It's a pity. Things are largely dependent on personal ties. Once the leader of the country changes, things won't work anymore. I don't think Kono has that much awareness, and Kishida also.

SHIO OKAWA

I don't think so, either.

IVAN IV

I don't think Takaichi has it, either. She'll just insist on taking back the Northern Territories.

SHIO OKAWA

Do you think so?

IVAN IV

They will all insist on that. So nothing will probably move forward. Even if we suggest that we set up a special economic zone, they will most probably hesitate to agree to that. Well...

Japan, in the first place, hasn't succeeded in settling the Takeshima issue before it can even fight against North Korea. The same goes for the Senkaku Islands.

Spiritual Message from Ivan IV, the First Tsar of Russia

SHIO OKAWA

Let me ask you the other way around. What kind of actions do you or Mr. Putin expect Japan to take for you to see the light?

IVAN IV

Well, as Master Ryuho Okawa said, even just saying, "Let's bring Russia back to the G8,"...

SHIO OKAWA

You would be thankful?

IVAN IV

Actually, I was very happy when he said that. It was what I hoped for.

Japanese people don't know anything about Ukraine. They have no clue. But Master Okawa understood it well. He knew that because of Ukraine's presence, Russia was able to win the wars against Napoleon and Hitler. No other person studies that much.

SHIO OKAWA

There's none.

Talking about the impression of the Biden administration

SHIO OKAWA
What kind of impression did you get by interacting with the Biden administration?

IVAN IV
Well, he's a populist, really.

SHIO OKAWA
Oh. A real populist.

IVAN IV
I mean, as a politician, I do understand him. But as a politician, you need to have a vision of what you want to achieve. And to realize that vision, you use all kinds of methods. But Mr. Biden is just trying to gain popularity.

SHIO OKAWA
That's his goal.

IVAN IV
Yes, that is his goal.

SHIO OKAWA

I see. He is just aiming to gain popularity.

IVAN IV

That's a corrupted version of democracy.

SHIO OKAWA

So, he is exposing the bad side of democracy.

IVAN IV

Yes, exactly.

SHIO OKAWA

In a way, he is showing us that.

IVAN IV

That's why the U.S. cannot firmly stand as an opposite axis.

SHIO OKAWA

Well, I understand he has been working on the human rights issue in China, though.

IVAN IV

But what can he do about it? He can't do anything.

SHIO OKAWA

That's true. After all, he has blurred the argument that coronavirus was leaked from the laboratory in Wuhan.

IVAN IV

I doubt he can do anything for Hong Kong and Taiwan as well.

SHIO OKAWA

It's doubtful if he can help them. Hong Kong is already losing now.

IVAN IV

The best thing he can do would be to protect the refugees.

India may develop more, but I think it's still difficult for them to counterbalance Russia as they are now. They are... well, India is still a little behind in westernization.

As for Japan, you probably think there's not much you can do now. I wish the Happiness Realization Party had flourished a little more.

SHIO OKAWA

Well, it's no use talking about it now. Japanese people still don't understand us enough.

Spiritual Message from Ivan IV, the First Tsar of Russia

IVAN IV

I truly wonder why those islands, which they have never visited themselves, are so important. Our schoolbooks write about them too. Well, Japanese people probably don't understand the difference between Russia and China.

SHIO OKAWA

Broadly speaking, people are still influenced strongly by materialism, and religion is often considered evil. Humanity has now become like a mass of people who feel more comfortable without God or Buddha. I think everyone prefers living without God or Buddha.

IVAN IV

It's true in some areas, but there are also places where it doesn't apply.

SHIO OKAWA

Of course, I'm sure there are still people with strong faith. But as I hear many opinions, including those of young people, I get the impression that more people want to live freely and think that the world would be more exciting if it had more rights and freedom.

The culprit of spreading the novel coronavirus

IVAN IV

It seems the coronavirus war is likely to end without identifying the culprit.

SHIO OKAWA

Yes, indeed. How does Russia see the coronavirus pandemic?

IVAN IV

China did it, of course [*laughs*].

SHIO OKAWA

Will you be in trouble if you say it openly?

IVAN IV

That's obvious, but it's no use saying it.

SHIO OKAWA

Hmm.

Spiritual Message from Ivan IV, the First Tsar of Russia

IVAN IV

It caused as many as 40 million people to get infected in the U.S. (at the time of the recording), so it's a great success for them. They're bursting into laughter and are having trouble hiding it.

SHIO OKAWA

But we must say it, rather than saying it's no use.

IVAN IV

China stirred things up by stating several theories, such as the virus originated in the U.S., it spread from overseas frozen foods, or it has a natural origin, and now, things got quieted down.

SHIO OKAWA

Don't you, Ivan IV, intend to say anything about that?

IVAN IV

Huh? There's no use. We have the issue of how to use China—whether or not we use China as Russia's shield. At the moment, they are not our potential enemy. China is a fake communist, though. It's clearly a fake communist nation. It's a corruption-ridden country.

4

About the Future of International Affairs

Concerns that the entire world might drift

SHIO OKAWA

As Tsar Ivan IV, what kind of world map are you aiming to achieve?

IVAN IV

I'm not the top leader in the world, so I'm not sure about that. But I don't want the U.S. to be hostile to Russia one-sidedly.

SHIO OKAWA

You don't intend to be hostile to the U.S., do you?

IVAN IV

No, it's the U.S. who gets hostile to us. They attack... or come against Russia.

SHIO OKAWA
That's done by Mr. Biden, right?

IVAN IV
He brings all the blame to Russia. He will say that everything is Russia's fault. So I want to make a breakthrough somehow.

I wanted to establish a friendly relationship with Japan during my term. I don't like China so much. I don't really want to do the same kind of politics the Chinese are doing. It's a pity that there was no brave leader (in Japan).

Europe will be troubled by another immigration issue. They will have a hard time from now.

SHIO OKAWA
Looking at how the people of Afghanistan are desperate to escape their own country, I feel truly sorry.

IVAN IV
The freedom of movement and residence is very important. It's hard to be unable to leave one's country.

SHIO OKAWA
The people of Hong Kong are also unable to leave their country now.

IVAN IV
No, they can't.

SHIO OKAWA
Especially the activists who were seeking freedom couldn't.

IVAN IV
If the U.S. were to act according to its original value judgment, it should be shooting a missile into the Hong Kong government offices. But they probably think such an act would be the same as what Russia has done to Ukraine. There's actually a different meaning, though.

SHIO OKAWA
Maybe the U.S. has changed somewhat after the Vietnam and Iraq wars. They may have lost confidence in their sense of justice.

IVAN IV

These wars caused a lot of casualties, and no one appreciates what the U.S. has done.

SHIO OKAWA

The other day was the 9/11 anniversary. It was most certainly Saudi Arabia who did it, but the U.S. attacked Iraq instead.

IVAN IV

Well, what to do from now on? I also wonder what Xi Jinping will do. I'm sure domestic problems will occur, too.

SHIO OKAWA

Do you mean in China?

IVAN IV

Yes.

SHIO OKAWA

What kind of problems do you think will occur?

IVAN IV

The economic gap is widening too much among the people in China.

SHIO OKAWA

I'm sure you have researched China a lot since Russia is good at doing such things. So I suppose many people are frustrated in China.

IVAN IV

Well... we may enter an age when the entire world becomes drifted. I think there is not much you can do, but you must lead the world in the right direction at any cost.

SHIO OKAWA

Even if we are in the minority, we must keep voicing our opinions and spreading Master Okawa's thinking.

IVAN IV

I'm sure Biden's true intention is to destroy Russia and also destroy the Islamic world.

SHIO OKAWA

But why does he hate Russia so much?

IVAN IV

Because his ideas are old fashioned.

SHIO OKAWA

Is that the only reason? So it's not like he holds personal grudges. It's just that his thinking has stopped at the olden times.

IVAN IV

Yes, it's outdated. It's old.

SHIO OKAWA

To him, America's potential enemy was Russia for the majority of his life, and his ideas haven't changed since then. Even though Russia did change, his idea about Russia hasn't been updated and is still old.

IVAN IV

Now, what should we do? You know, the U.K. will split again.

SHIO OKAWA

Ms. Merkel of Germany will be replaced soon (at the time of the recording). Germany may also change, depending on the kind of person the next chancellor will be.

IVAN IV

Germany is also too pitiful after World War II. Now that the U.K. has left, the EU will be terrible if Germany weakens. China could overrun it.

Warning against Biden's foreign policy toward Asia

IVAN IV

The reason why I came here today is that I'm hoping that you will include the Russian issues in your (publication) strategy, translate and publish them in English-speaking countries if the opportunity arises. Japanese people will probably feel a strong affinity with me if they hear that I had a very close relationship with the Sun Goddess Amaterasu-O-Mikami (in my other past lives).

SHIO OKAWA

Yes. And President Putin does judo as well.

IVAN IV

Yes. I wish Mr. Abe had had a "bold strategy" against Russia.

SHIO OKAWA

In the end, he sought to leave his name by the number of days he stayed in office instead of the quality of the work he did.

IVAN IV

Hmm... [*Five seconds of silence.*] The U.S. hasn't done anything for Myanmar either, right?

SHIO OKAWA

That's true.

IVAN IV

You know, Biden is bad at diplomacy, although he claims he is good at it.

SHIO OKAWA

He is all talk.

IVAN IV

He is actually bad at diplomacy and doesn't understand anything about it. He doesn't understand the relationship between the Philippines and China. He doesn't understand

Thailand either. He basically doesn't understand anything. So, it is highly likely that Japan will truly become a battlefield if the present situation were to continue. You must be cautious, seriously.

SHIO OKAWA

I feel Mr. Biden is really like a Japanese, especially looking at his ways of thinking.

IVAN IV

I don't know. I shouldn't say anything about what he doesn't say himself.

SHIO OKAWA

That's true. It may bring about more hostility should anything happen. I'm sorry.

IVAN IV

To say the least, Japan must try harder because Southeast Asia has also been rocked.

SHIO OKAWA

I understand.

IVAN IV

There are many Japanese factories in China. If something suddenly happens to them... Well, but the Japanese companies probably believe that everything will go back to normal when the coronavirus pandemic settles down.

SHIO OKAWA

I think so. Companies like UNIQLO must be thinking that way.

IVAN IV

And Toyota also. I'm not sure if everything will be back to normal, though. I don't know if Japan can even develop in its own way, either. Japan was like a suckerfish on the U.S., but the U.S. is now falling rapidly from being an advanced nation to a second-class nation.

SHIO OKAWA

Yes, it's starting to fall.

IVAN IV

It's been largely regressed in just six months or so, right?

SHIO OKAWA
Yes.

IVAN IV
After all, the leader needs to be wise to some extent.

5

Thoughts on Russia's Relations with Japan and China

Views on Iran and Israel

SHIO OKAWA

I think Japan's educational system can no longer produce wise people. Unless people study hard by themselves, they can't truly be wise.

IVAN IV

It must be difficult. I wish I had a reliable counterpart to negotiate with in Japan, but that's difficult for now. It seems to me that Master Okawa is starting to think of focusing on religious work and fulfilling his mission and destiny.

SHIO OKAWA

We need to leave behind the religious teachings. His teachings will guide the people of the future, so it's important work. No matter what happens in politics, we must leave behind the teachings on how to live and think as human beings.

IVAN IV

Hmm... If I continue like this, China will become jealous, so I will stop by now.

SHIO OKAWA

Will China be jealous?

IVAN IV

Yes, they will be jealous.

SHIO OKAWA

About what?

IVAN IV

Huh? I mean, China will be jealous if Japan considers treating Russia favorably.

SHIO OKAWA

Oh, I see. China gets jealous.

IVAN IV

Yes. It would be best if China dug its own grave. [*About five seconds of silence.*] Well...

SHIO OKAWA

I heard that Tsar Ivan IV was unable to sleep well at night during his life. It's probably the same in this lifetime, too, I'm afraid.

IVAN IV

Well, there is not much I can do. But it's natural to return a favor, you know? If only there was…

SHIO OKAWA

Some connection?

IVAN IV

I am hoping that you will be the bridge somehow. We are quite aware of your presence. We understand that the Happiness Realization Party, or Happy Science, shows a certain level of understanding toward Russia.

The movement of Iran and Israel and other factors are making things more difficult. If you are running out of good measures, then it means we have no more measures to take either.

SHIO OKAWA

We can understand Iran's position in some respects, but with their current regime, they are very close to totalitarianism. So, it's true that Iran needs to make some innovations.

IVAN IV

Hmm...

Ah [*sighs*]. Well, I just came here to tell you what I'm thinking. But I don't have any solutions, and it seems like neither do you.

SHIO OKAWA

There aren't any solutions if things remain as they are now.

IVAN IV

At the moment, you're giving off a feeling of a simple housewife who doesn't want to get involved.

Spiritual Message from Ivan IV, the First Tsar of Russia

The U.S. may drop off from being a superpower if it cannot fight back against China

SHIO OKAWA
Anyway, the moment Mr. Biden became the U.S. president, we had no choice but to endure at least the next four years. Japan has got stuck and can't do anything.

IVAN IV
The world fell right into China's strategy. China worked to get Biden elected, thinking it would change everything, and in fact, it did.

SHIO OKAWA
The U.S. is split into roughly two groups, but the overwhelming majority seeks to expand human rights.

IVAN IV
What has expanded is not human rights but coronavirus to make Trump lose. They mainly targeted New York.

SHIO OKAWA
That's right. If it hadn't been for the coronavirus pandemic, Mr. Trump would have naturally been elected.

IVAN IV

He wouldn't have lost.

SHIO OKAWA

His approval ratings showed that.

IVAN IV

They (China) attacked New York to make Trump lose. So, if the U.S. can't fight back and puts an end to the matter without clarifying the reason at all, the U.S. will drop off from being a superpower of its own accord.

SHIO OKAWA

The media got on board, too.

IVAN IV

It has nothing to do with vaccines. They're just making excuses. It's not about vaccines. New variants are coming out one after another, so you can't make it with vaccines. They won't work.

The world is now headed for chaos, and unless the U.S. shows stronger determination, this can't be helped. Well, it is what the American people chose, so they must accept the consequence.

Spiritual Message from Ivan IV, the First Tsar of Russia

The mistake Japan was able to correct due to the coronavirus pandemic

SHIO OKAWA

Overall, everything has unfolded just as Master Okawa predicted through lectures and spiritual messages...

IVAN IV

We've translated them and read them quite a bit.

SHIO OKAWA

...that the world would be in confusion, in chaos, and become drifted from now on.

IVAN IV

There's nothing good. Well, I understand that creating too many enemies will make things even worse. To be more specific, at some point soon, they will break through Hong Kong, for example.

SHIO OKAWA

Do you mean China?

IVAN IV

They are preparing for it. China will probably send its raiding forces into the Hong Kong administration and seize everything in the end. They will contain it by preventing its people from escaping from the coast. The world's third-largest financial city will be lost. But I guess it's OK for them because they probably think of using Macau instead.

In exchange, China tried to colonize Japan. To achieve that, they sent tourists and made them buy land and do lots of shopping in Japan. In this way, they tried to make Japanese people come to like China. In the past, I think about 70 percent of Japanese people had good feelings toward China.

SHIO OKAWA

The number has been decreasing.

IVAN IV

It's about 20 percent now.

SHIO OKAWA

But if coronavirus hadn't spread in Japan, China's influence would have become greater at an earlier stage.

Even Mr. Abe was welcoming Chinese tourists, and he was thinking of achieving economic recovery by relying mainly on China.

IVAN IV
It was good that that mistake was corrected.

SHIO OKAWA
It was at least postponed.

IVAN IV
Hmm... For the time being, I can only think of ways to maintain my administration as long as possible.

SHIO OKAWA
You are figuring it out.

IVAN IV
While seeing Japan's leader changing every year, and before you know it, there's no one left to negotiate with. That's why I've come here (Happy Science) to ask.

Thoughts on Japan's response to the Four Northern Islands, Takeshima, and Senkaku Islands

IVAN IV

Well, hmm... What can I say...

Maybe you are trying to shift your attention more to day-to-day affairs.

SHIO OKAWA

But this situation in Japan is also exactly the same as what was predicted in Master Okawa's lectures. No brakes had worked.

IVAN IV

Indeed, nothing changes.

SHIO OKAWA

Nothing changes, so it can't be helped. We can only work on our activities steadily without giving up.

IVAN IV

Maybe Japan is making an effort to increase disaster-relief work for its Self-Defense Forces, no?

Spiritual Message from Ivan IV, the First Tsar of Russia

SHIO OKAWA

Things are moving, just as Master Okawa said, so I'm not really surprised. He has also already predicted that Japan's prime ministers will change one after another.

IVAN IV

Master Ryuho Okawa is the only person in Japan who has suggested that Japan restore diplomatic relations with Russia (by signing the Peace Treaty) even at the cost of the Four Northern Islands because those islands won't bring many benefits to Japan. Everyone else is so desperate for those islands.

SHIO OKAWA

It's strange that Japan is overly obsessed with the northern islands when they normally act as if they don't mind losing islands (in other areas).

IVAN IV

Why don't you get angry at the fact that Takeshima is occupied?

SHIO OKAWA

It's a mystery why Japan is so obsessed with the Northern Territories.

IVAN IV

I don't understand why Japan doesn't build a base on the Senkaku Islands when China claims these islands are their core interest.

SHIO OKAWA

Well, Japan is a little off with when to be stubborn or not.

IVAN IV

Unless Japan builds the base, it can't claim sovereignty over the islands. So they can't say anything even if these islands are suddenly taken.

SHIO OKAWA

Japanese people don't like to rock the boat. They believe that if they don't take action, their counterpart won't either. But China has been taking action in reality. They are violating our airspace and intruding on our territorial waters.

IVAN IV

I think it has something to do with coronavirus being relatively widespread in Okinawa. China intends to take it too.

But it seems that China's vaccine diplomacy has failed. Different countries use Chinese vaccines, and they all say they don't work. It's strange that they work perfectly only in China, isn't it?

SHIO OKAWA

I wonder if people really don't die (of coronavirus) or get infected in China. How are they hiding it?

IVAN IV

China has the power to control information. I don't know if this means they have modernized. Anyway, there is no doubt that they are trying hard to brainwash their people. In a sense, China is the largest "religious" nation in the world.

What will become of the U.S. forces in Japan under the Biden administration?

SHIO OKAWA

There is one more thing Master mentioned about China. Recently, Xi Jinping has been increasingly cutting back English education in China.

IVAN IV

Well, I'm not surprised to hear that.

SHIO OKAWA

But if they do that, they will inevitably become even more insensitive to international affairs.

IVAN IV

That's right.

SHIO OKAWA

So, although they take a strong attitude, they may be digging their own hole somewhere.

IVAN IV

As long as the Japanese companies operate in China, they will be finished if China takes over their factories. Since over 90 percent of the employees are probably locals, even if they stop operating for the sake of the Uyghurs, the Uyghurs are the only ones to suffer. It will only take away their source of income. So there is nothing good in doing that.

I myself have Western values in my mind. But in reality, what I will have to do may appear similar to what

China is doing. This may not sound good, but I wish Russia was decoupled (from China).

SHIO OKAWA
Well, that's what Master has been saying all along.

IVAN IV
At least, I wanted the freedom to visit and pay respect to the memorial places of Master Jigoro Kano (known as the father of judo) from time to time.

Hmm... This all started from America's ignorance, so it can't be helped. Regardless of what happens to the U.S., I think Japan had better come up with measures to survive. I'm serious. If Biden is left in charge, all the countries with nuclear weapons may start to set their eyes on Japan. A real caller of misfortune, indeed.

SHIO OKAWA
Do you mean Mr. Biden?

IVAN IV
Yes.

SHIO OKAWA

Why does he appear like a nice guy to everyone?

IVAN IV

If the nuclear weapons are all aimed at Japan...

SHIO OKAWA

Oh, it will help America.

IVAN IV

The U.S. forces in Japan can then be withdrawn. They can retreat as far back as Hawaii. I think that's what he's really after.

SHIO OKAWA

Oh, I see. So, Mr. Biden wants to make a withdrawal, too.

IVAN IV

That's because the U.S. suffers a fiscal deficit. He wants to retreat the military more and more. I think they will retreat as far back as Hawaii. I'm even skeptical if they would keep Guam as well.

The end of the American superpower itself is good in some sense, but who will lead the world after that is a difficult matter. I hope the Happiness Realization Party will have more power.

SHIO OKAWA
Thank you for having expectations of us. Shall we end the interview here?

IVAN IV
OK.

SHIO OKAWA
Please take care of yourself.

IVAN IV
Thank you.

TRANSLATOR'S NOTE

1 (Taro) Kono, (Sanae) Takaichi

Taro Kono and Sanae Takaichi were the candidates for the Liberal Democratic Party leadership election in 2021. It was taking place during the current recording. Fumio Kishida won the election in late September and became the prime minister.

Afterword

The spiritual message from one of President Putin's past lives, Ivan IV, was added for reference.

The collapse of the Soviet Union more than 30 years ago must have been miserable. President Putin has spent the last 20 years trying to revive the Great Russian Empire.

My opinion is different from the mass media in the world or in Japan. I don't think Ukraine should join the EU. It was thanks to Ukraine that Russia (the Soviet Union) eventually won the Napoleonic Wars and the war against Hitler even after Moscow was burned to the ground. It would be a nightmare for Russia if American nuclear missiles were placed in Ukraine to be launched against Moscow. President Putin is decisive. I knew that he would not tolerate that.

The decision-making skill of the top leaders will change the course of the world from now on. For Mr. Biden, this is the second war he has lost, following the war against coronavirus. It is unfortunate, but he is just brainless.

Ryuho Okawa
Master & CEO of Happy Science Group
February 26, 2022

For a deeper understanding of
Putin's Real Intentions on Ukraine Invasion
see other books below by Ryuho Okawa:

A New Message from Vladimir Putin [Tokyo: HS Press, 2014]
Shakyamuni Buddha's Future Prediction [Tokyo: HS Press, 2020]
What Will Become of Coronavirus Pandemic? [Tokyo: HS Press, 2020]
Spiritual Interviews with the Guardian Spirits of Biden and Trump [Tokyo: HS Press, 2020]
Spiritual Messages from Yaidron: Save the World from Destruction [Tokyo: HS Press, 2021]
Trump Shall Never Die [Tokyo: HS Press, 2021]
Inside the Mind of President Biden [Tokyo: HS Press, 2021]

ABOUT THE AUTHOR

RYUHO OKAWA was born on July 7th 1956, in Tokushima, Japan. After graduating from the University of Tokyo with a law degree, he joined a Tokyo-based trading house. While working at its New York headquarters, he studied international finance at the Graduate Center of the City University of New York. In 1981, he attained Great Enlightenment and became aware that he is El Cantare with a mission to bring salvation to all humankind. In 1986, he established Happy Science. It now has members in over 160 countries across the world, with more than 700 branches and temples as well as 10,000 missionary houses around the world. The total number of lectures has exceeded 3,400 (of which more than 150 are in English) and over 2,950 books (of which more than 600 are Spiritual Interview Series) have been published, many of which are translated into 37 languages. Many of the books, including *The Laws of the Sun* have become best sellers or million sellers. To date, Happy Science has produced 25 movies. The original story and original concept were given by the Executive Producer Ryuho Okawa. Recent movie titles are *The Laws of the Universe - The Age of Elohim* (animation movie, October 2021), *The Cherry Bushido* (live-action movie, February 2022), *The Divine Protector-Master Salt Begins* (live-action movie scheduled to be released in Fall of 2022). He has also composed the lyrics and music of over 450 songs, such as theme songs and featured songs of movies. Moreover, he is the Founder of Happy Science University and Happy Science Academy (Junior and Senior High School), Founder and President of the Happiness Realization Party, Founder and Honorary Headmaster of Happy Science Institute of Government and Management, Founder of IRH Press Co., Ltd., and the Chairperson of NEW STAR PRODUCTION Co., Ltd. and ARI Production Co., Ltd.

WHAT IS EL CANTARE?

El Cantare means "the Light of the Earth," and is the Supreme God of the Earth who has been guiding humankind since the beginning of Genesis. He is whom Jesus called Father and Muhammad called Allah, and is *Ame-no-Mioya-Gami*, Japanese Father God. Different parts of El Cantare's core consciousness have descended to Earth in the past, once as Alpha and another as Elohim. His branch spirits, such as Shakyamuni Buddha and Hermes, have descended to Earth many times and helped to flourish many civilizations. To unite various religions and to integrate various fields of study in order to build a new civilization on Earth, a part of the core consciousness has descended to Earth as Master Ryuho Okawa.

Alpha is a part of the core consciousness of El Cantare who descended to Earth around 330 million years ago. Alpha preached Earth's Truths to harmonize and unify Earth-born humans and space people who came from other planets.

Elohim is a part of El Cantare's core consciousness who descended to Earth around 150 million years ago. He gave wisdom, mainly on the differences of light and darkness, good and evil.

Ame-no-Mioya-Gami (Japanese Father God) is the Creator God and the Father God who appears in the ancient literature, *Hotsuma Tsutae*. It is believed that He descended on the foothills of Mt. Fuji about 30,000 years ago and built the Fuji dynasty, which is the root of the Japanese civilization. With justice as the central pillar, Ame-no-Mioya-Gami's teachings spread to ancient civilizations of other countries in the world.

Shakyamuni Buddha was born as a prince into the Shakya Clan in India around 2,600 years ago. When he was 29 years old, he renounced the world and sought enlightenment. He later attained Great Enlightenment and founded Buddhism.

Hermes is one of the 12 Olympian gods in Greek mythology, but the spiritual Truth is that he taught the teachings of love and progress around 4,300 years ago that became the origin of the current Western civilization. He is a hero that truly existed.

Ophealis was born in Greece around 6,500 years ago and was the leader who took an expedition to as far as Egypt. He is the God of miracles, prosperity, and arts, and is known as Osiris in the Egyptian mythology.

Rient Arl Croud was born as a king of the ancient Incan Empire around 7,000 years ago and taught about the mysteries of the mind. In the heavenly world, he is responsible for the interactions that take place between various planets.

Thoth was an almighty leader who built the golden age of the Atlantic civilization around 12,000 years ago. In the Egyptian mythology, he is known as god Thoth.

Ra Mu was a leader who built the golden age of the civilization of Mu around 17,000 years ago. As a religious leader and a politician, he ruled by uniting religion and politics.

WHAT IS A SPIRITUAL MESSAGE?

We are all spiritual beings living on this earth. The following is the mechanism behind Master Ryuho Okawa's spiritual messages.

1 You are a spirit

People are born into this world to gain wisdom through various experiences and return to the other world when their lives end. We are all spirits and repeat this cycle in order to refine our souls.

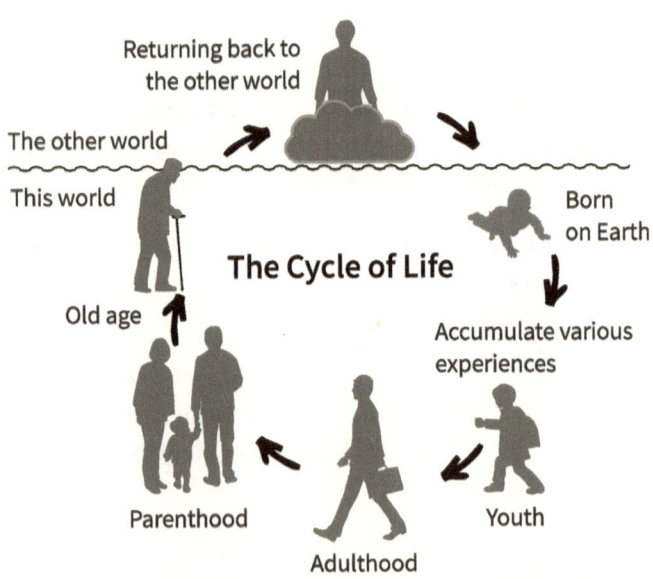

2 You have a guardian spirit

Guardian spirits are those who protect the people who are living on this earth. Each of us has a guardian spirit that watches over us and guides us from the other world. They were us in our past life, and are identical in how we think.

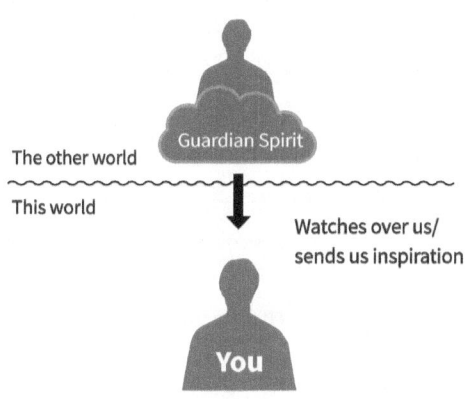

3 How spiritual messages work

Master Ryuho Okawa, through his enlightenment, is capable of summoning any spirit from anywhere in the world, including the spirit world.

Master Okawa's way of receiving spiritual messages is fundamentally different from that of other psychic mediums who undergo trances and are thereby completely taken over by the spirits they are channeling.

Master Okawa's attainment of a high level of enlightenment enables him to retain full control of his consciousness and body throughout the duration of the spiritual message. To allow the spirits to express their own thoughts and personalities freely, however, Master Okawa usually softens the dominancy of his consciousness. This way, he is able to keep his own philosophies out of the way and ensure that the spiritual messages are pure expressions of the spirits he is channeling.

Since guardian spirits think at the same subconscious level as the person living on earth, Master Okawa can summon the spirit and find out what the person on earth is actually thinking. If the person has already returned to the other world, the spirit can give messages to the people living on earth through Master Okawa.

Since 2009, many spiritual messages have been openly recorded by Master Okawa and published. Spiritual messages from the guardian spirits of people living today such as Donald Trump, former Japanese Prime Minister Shinzo Abe and Chinese President Xi Jinping, as well as spiritual messages sent from the spirit world by Jesus Christ, Muhammad, Thomas Edison, Mother Teresa, Steve Jobs and Nelson Mandela are just a tiny pack of spiritual messages that were published so far.

Domestically, in Japan, these spiritual messages are being read by a wide range of politicians and mass media, and the high-level contents of these books are delivering an impact even more on politics, news and public opinion. In recent years, there have been spiritual messages recorded in English, and

English translations are being done on the spiritual messages given in Japanese. These have been published overseas, one after another, and have started to shake the world.

1. The guardian spirit / spirit in the other world...
2. Goes inside Master Okawa in this world
3. Master Okawa speaks the words of the guardian spirit / spirit

For more about spiritual messages and a complete list of books in the Spiritual Interview Series, visit okawabooks.com

ABOUT HAPPY SCIENCE

Happy Science is a global movement that empowers individuals to find purpose and spiritual happiness and to share that happiness with their families, societies, and the world. With more than 12 million members around the world, Happy Science aims to increase awareness of spiritual truths and expand our capacity for love, compassion, and joy so that together we can create the kind of world we all wish to live in.

Activities at Happy Science are based on the Principle of Happiness (Love, Wisdom, Self-Reflection, and Progress). This principle embraces worldwide philosophies and beliefs, transcending boundaries of culture and religions.

Love teaches us to give ourselves freely without expecting anything in return; it encompasses giving, nurturing, and forgiving.

Wisdom leads us to the insights of spiritual truths, and opens us to the true meaning of life and the will of God (the universe, the highest power, Buddha).

Self-Reflection brings a mindful, nonjudgmental lens to our thoughts and actions to help us find our truest selves—the essence of our souls—and deepen our connection to the highest power. It helps us attain a clean and peaceful mind and leads us to the right life path.

Progress emphasizes the positive, dynamic aspects of our spiritual growth—actions we can take to manifest and spread happiness around the world. It's a path that not only expands our soul growth, but also furthers the collective potential of the world we live in.

PROGRAMS AND EVENTS

The doors of Happy Science are open to all. We offer a variety of programs and events, including self-exploration and self-growth programs, spiritual seminars, meditation and contemplation sessions, study groups, and book events.

Our programs are designed to:
* Deepen your understanding of your purpose and meaning in life
* Improve your relationships and increase your capacity to love unconditionally
* Attain peace of mind, decrease anxiety and stress, and feel positive
* Gain deeper insights and a broader perspective on the world
* Learn how to overcome life's challenges
    ... and much more.

For more information, visit happy-science.org.

CONTACT INFORMATION

Happy Science is a worldwide organization with branches and temples around the globe. For a comprehensive list, visit the worldwide directory at *happy-science.org*. The following are some of the many Happy Science locations:

UNITED STATES AND CANADA

New York
79 Franklin St., New York, NY 10013, USA
Phone: 1-212-343-7972
Fax: 1-212-343-7973
Email: ny@happy-science.org
Website: happyscience-usa.org

New Jersey
66 Hudson St., #2R, Hoboken, NJ 07030, USA
Phone: 1-201-313-0127
Email: nj@happy-science.org
Website: happyscience-usa.org

Chicago
2300 Barrington Rd., Suite #400,
Hoffman Estates, IL 60169, USA
Phone: 1-630-937-3077
Email: chicago@happy-science.org
Website: happyscience-usa.org

Florida
5208 8th St., Zephyrhills, FL 33542, USA
Phone: 1-813-715-0000
Fax: 1-813-715-0010
Email: florida@happy-science.org
Website: happyscience-usa.org

Atlanta
1874 Piedmont Ave., NE Suite 360-C
Atlanta, GA 30324, USA
Phone: 1-404-892-7770
Email: atlanta@happy-science.org
Website: happyscience-usa.org

San Francisco
525 Clinton St.
Redwood City, CA 94062, USA
Phone & Fax: 1-650-363-2777
Email: sf@happy-science.org
Website: happyscience-usa.org

Los Angeles
1590 E. Del Mar Blvd., Pasadena, CA 91106, USA
Phone: 1-626-395-7775
Fax: 1-626-395-7776
Email: la@happy-science.org
Website: happyscience-usa.org

Orange County
16541 Gothard St. Suite 104
Huntington Beach, CA 92647
Phone: 1-714-659-1501
Email: oc@happy-science.org
Website: happyscience-usa.org

San Diego
7841 Balboa Ave. Suite #202
San Diego, CA 92111, USA
Phone: 1-626-395-7775
Fax: 1-626-395-7776
E-mail: sandiego@happy-science.org
Website: happyscience-usa.org

Hawaii
Phone: 1-808-591-9772
Fax: 1-808-591-9776
Email: hi@happy-science.org
Website: happyscience-usa.org

Kauai
3343 Kanakolu Street, Suite 5
Lihue, HI 96766, USA
Phone: 1-808-822-7007
Fax: 1-808-822-6007
Email: kauai-hi@happy-science.org
Website: happyscience-usa.org

Toronto
845 The Queensway
Etobicoke, ON M8Z 1N6, Canada
Phone: 1-416-901-3747
Email: toronto@happy-science.org
Website: happy-science.ca

Vancouver
#201-2607 East 49th Avenue,
Vancouver, BC, V5S 1J9, Canada
Phone: 1-604-437-7735
Fax: 1-604-437-7764
Email: vancouver@happy-science.org
Website: happy-science.ca

INTERNATIONAL

Tokyo
1-6-7 Togoshi, Shinagawa,
Tokyo, 142-0041, Japan
Phone: 81-3-6384-5770
Fax: 81-3-6384-5776
Email: tokyo@happy-science.org
Website: happy-science.org

Seoul
74, Sadang-ro 27-gil,
Dongjak-gu, Seoul, Korea
Phone: 82-2-3478-8777
Fax: 82-2-3478-9777
Email: korea@happy-science.org
Website: happyscience-korea.org

London
3 Margaret St.
London, W1W 8RE United Kingdom
Phone: 44-20-7323-9255
Fax: 44-20-7323-9344
Email: eu@happy-science.org
Website: www.happyscience-uk.org

Taipei
No. 89, Lane 155, Dunhua N. Road,
Songshan District, Taipei City 105, Taiwan
Phone: 886-2-2719-9377
Fax: 886-2-2719-5570
Email: taiwan@happy-science.org
Website: happyscience-tw.org

Sydney
516 Pacific Highway, Lane Cove North,
2066 NSW, Australia
Phone: 61-2-9411-2877
Fax: 61-2-9411-2822
Email: sydney@happy-science.org

Kuala Lumpur
No 22A, Block 2, Jalil Link Jalan Jalil
Jaya 2, Bukit Jalil 57000,
Kuala Lumpur, Malaysia
Phone: 60-3-8998-7877
Fax: 60-3-8998-7977
Email: malaysia@happy-science.org
Website: happyscience.org.my

Sao Paulo
Rua. Domingos de Morais 1154,
Vila Mariana, Sao Paulo SP
CEP 04010-100, Brazil
Phone: 55-11-5088-3800
Email: sp@happy-science.org
Website: happyscience.com.br

Kathmandu
Kathmandu Metropolitan City,
Ward No. 15, Ring Road, Kimdol,
Sitapaila Kathmandu, Nepal
Phone: 977-1-427-2931
Email: nepal@happy-science.org

Jundiai
Rua Congo, 447, Jd. Bonfiglioli
Jundiai-CEP, 13207-340, Brazil
Phone: 55-11-4587-5952
Email: jundiai@happy-science.org

Kampala
Plot 877 Rubaga Road, Kampala
P.O. Box 34130 Kampala, UGANDA
Phone: 256-79-4682-121
Email: uganda@happy-science.org

ABOUT HS PRESS

HS Press is an imprint of IRH Press Co., Ltd. IRH Press Co., Ltd., based in Tokyo, was founded in 1987 as a publishing division of Happy Science. IRH Press publishes religious and spiritual books, journals, magazines and also operates broadcast and film production enterprises. For more information, visit *okawabooks.com*.

Follow us on:

- Facebook: Okawa Books
- Youtube: Okawa Books
- Pinterest: Okawa Books
- Instagram: OkawaBooks
- Twitter: Okawa Books
- Goodreads: Ryuho Okawa

--- **NEWSLETTER** ---

To receive book related news, promotions and events, please subscribe to our newsletter below.

eepurl.com/bsMeJj

AUDIO / VISUAL MEDIA

YOUTUBE

PODCAST

Introduction of Ryuho Okawa's titles; topics ranging from self-help, current affairs, spirituality, religion, and the universe.

BOOKS BY RYUHO OKAWA

RYUHO OKAWA'S LAWS SERIES

The Laws Series is an annual volume of books that are mainly comprised of Ryuho Okawa's lectures that function as universal guidance to all people. They are of various topics that were given in accordance with the changes that each year brings. *The Laws of the Sun*, the first publication of the laws series, ranked in the annual best-selling list in Japan in 1994. Since, the laws series' titles have ranked in the annual best-selling list every year for more than two decades, setting socio-cultural trends in Japan and around the world.

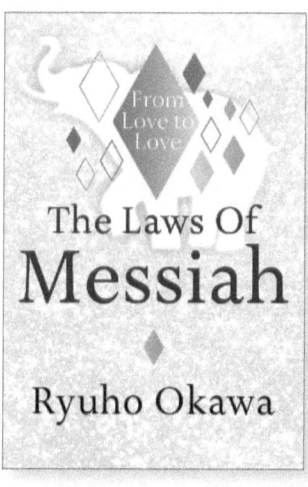

The 28th Laws Series
The Laws Of Messiah
From Love to Love
Paperback • 248 pages • $16.95
ISBN: 978-1-942125-90-7 (Jan. 31, 2022)

"What is Messiah?" This book carries an important message of love and guidance to people living now from the Modern-Day Messiah or the Modern-Day Savior. It also reveals the secret of Shambhala, the spiritual center of Earth, as well as the truth that this spiritual center is currently in danger of perishing and what we can do to protect this sacred place.

Love your Lord God. Know that those who don't know love don't know God. Discover the true love of God and the ideal practice of faith. This book teaches the most important element we must not lose sight of as we go through our soul training on Earth.

For a complete list of books, visit okawabooks.com

TO CULTIVATE EL CANTARE FAITH

THE TEN PRINCIPLES
FROM EL CANTARE VOLUME I

RYUHO OKAWA'S FIRST LECTURES
ON HIS BASIC TEACHINGS

Paperback • 232 pages • $16.95
ISBN: 978-1-942125-85-3 (Dec. 6, 2021)

This book contains the historic lectures given on the first five principles of the Ten Principles of Happy Science from the author, Ryuho Okawa, who is revered as World Teacher. These lectures produced an enthusiastic fellowship in Happy Science Japan and became the foundation of the current global utopian movement. You can learn the essence of Okawa's teachings and the secret behind the rapid growth of the Happy Science movement in simple language.

For a complete list of books, visit <u>okawabooks.com</u>

Scheduled to be published in April 2022.

THE TEN PRINCIPLES FROM EL CANTARE VOLUME II

RYUHO OKAWA'S FIRST LECTURES ON HIS WISH TO SAVE THE WORLD

Paperback • 272 pages • $16.95
ISBN: 978-1-942125-86-0

A sequel to *The Ten Principles from El Cantare Volume I*. Volume II reveals the Creator's three major inventions; the secret of the creation of human souls, the meaning of time, and 'happiness' as life's purpose. By reading this book, you can not only improve yourself but learn how to make differences in society and create an ideal, utopian world.

For a complete list of books, visit okawabooks.com

THE TRILOGY

The first three volumes of the Laws Series, *The Laws of the Sun*, *The Golden Laws*, and *The Nine Dimensions* make a trilogy that completes the basic framework of the teachings of God's Truths. *The Laws of the Sun* discusses the structure of God's Laws, *The Golden Laws* expounds on the doctrine of time, and *The Nine Dimensions* reveals the nature of space.

THE LAWS OF THE SUN

ONE SOURCE, ONE PLANET, ONE PEOPLE

Paperback • 288 pages • $15.95
ISBN: 978-1-942125-43-3 (Oct. 15, 2018)

IMAGINE IF YOU COULD ASK GOD why He created this world and what spiritual laws He used to shape us—and everything around us. If we could understand His designs and intentions, we could discover what our goals in life should be and whether our actions move us closer to those goals or farther away.

At a young age, a spiritual calling prompted Ryuho Okawa to outline what he innately understood to be universal truths for all humankind. In *The Laws of the Sun*, Okawa outlines these laws of the universe and provides a road map for living one's life with greater purpose and meaning.

In this powerful book, Ryuho Okawa reveals the transcendent nature of consciousness and the secrets of our multidimensional universe and our place in it. By understanding the different stages of love and following the Buddhist Eightfold Path, he believes we can speed up our eternal process of development. *The Laws of the Sun* shows the way to realize true happiness—a happiness that continues from this world through the other.

THE GOLDEN LAWS
HISTORY THROUGH THE EYES OF THE ETERNAL BUDDHA

Paperback • 201 pages • $14.95
ISBN: 978-1-941779-81-1 (Jul. 1, 2011)

Throughout history, Great Guiding Spirits have been present on Earth in both the East and the West at crucial points in human history to further our spiritual development. *The Golden Laws* reveals how Divine Plan has been unfolding on Earth, and outlines 5,000 years of the secret history of humankind. Once we understand the true course of history, through past, present and into the future, we cannot help but become aware of the significance of our spiritual mission in the present age.

THE NINE DIMENSIONS
UNVEILING THE LAWS OF ETERNITY

Paperback • 168 pages • $15.95
ISBN: 978-0-982698-56-3 (Feb. 16, 2012)

This book is a window into the mind of our loving God, who designed this world and the vast, wondrous world of our afterlife as a school with many levels through which our souls learn and grow. When the religions and cultures of the world discover the truth of their common spiritual origin, they will be inspired to accept their differences, come together under faith in God, and build an era of harmony and peaceful progress on Earth.

For a complete list of books, visit okawabooks.com

WORLD POLITICAL LEADERS

TRUMP SHALL NEVER DIE
HIS DETERMINATION TO COME BACK

Paperback • 206 pages • $11.95
ISBN: 978-1-943928-08-8 (May 18, 2021)

What was the 2020 presidential election all about? What was Mr. Trump fighting for? And what was it that he aimed to achieve during his presidency? By reading this book, you will have a clear picture of how Mr. Trump sees the world situation and also realize how the world now needs true leaders who can think about world justice.

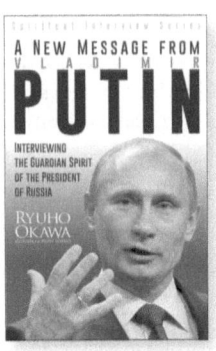

A NEW MESSAGE FROM VLADIMIR PUTIN
INTERVIEWING THE GUARDIAN SPIRIT OF THE PRESIDENT OF RUSSIA

Paperback • 232 pages • $14.95
ISBN: 978-1-937673-94-9 (Jun. 17, 2014)

We hereby bring you the spiritual message from the guardian spirit of President Putin, the politician who is the center of attention of not just the people of Russia but of the whole world, regardless of it being in a good or a bad way. In the Preface, it says, "President Putin's true intentions, which are 90 percent misunderstood."

INSIDE THE MIND OF PRESIDENT BIDEN
THOUGHTS REVEALED BY HIS GUARDIAN SPIRIT DAYS BEFORE HIS INAUGURATION

Paperback • 296 pages • $13.95
ISBN: 978-1-943928-02-6 (Mar. 2, 2021)

What are the real thoughts inside the mind of President Biden? What scheme does he know about the coronavirus crisis and the Obama administration's close ties with Beijing? You'll discover whether he can truly fulfill the responsibilities of an American president and a major world leader and also about the way he views the battle between democracy and totalitarianism we are now witnessing.

For a complete list of books, visit okawabooks.com

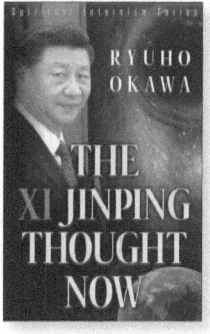

THE XI JINPING THOUGHT NOW

Paperback • 212 pages • $13.95
ISBN: 978-1-943928-05-7 (Apr. 16, 2021)

With the launch of Biden administration in the U.S. and the 100th anniversary of the founding of the Chinese Communist Party approaching, China has been expanding its military threat and reinforcing its influence over the world. What urges China to seek global hegemony? This book unveils the "dark being" behind the Xi Jinping Thought.

WILL THERE BE PEACE IN MYANMAR?

SPIRITUAL INTERVIEWS WITH THE GUARDIAN SPIRITS OF AUNG SAN SUU KYI AND GEN. MIN AUNG HLAING AND MESSAGES FROM SHAKYAMUNI BUDDHA

Paperback • 194 pages • $11.95
ISBN: 978-1-943928-12-5 (Aug. 4, 2021)

February 2021. Tatmadaw, Myanmar Armed Forces, staged a coup against the pro-democracy leader Aung San Suu Kyi. Behind the nation's army lurks one of the world's major powers working to gain its influence on Myanmar. But, now is the time for the world to change. Words from Shakyamuni Buddha will also help bring peace to Myanmar, Asia, and the world.

SPIRITUAL INTERVIEWS WITH THE GUARDIAN SPIRITS OF BIDEN AND TRUMP

Paperback • 200 pages • $11.95
ISBN: 978-1-943869-92-3 (Aug. 29, 2020)

The 2020 U.S. presidential election will be a turning point in history. In this book, we spiritually closed in on the true thoughts of Biden and Trump to get a forecast of the presidential election. In short, China could become the next hegemonic state if Biden is elected the president. Who you vote for could change people's lives, for better or worse.

For a complete list of books, visit okawabooks.com

CHOOSE LOVE BEYOND HATRED

THE LAWS OF JUSTICE
HOW WE CAN SOLVE WORLD CONFLICTS & BRING PEACE

Paperback • 224 pages • $15.95
ISBN: 978-1-942125-05-1 (Sep. 1, 2016)

How can we resolve conflicts in this world? Why do we live in constant turmoil, when we strive for peace? By contemplating this macro-view, it elevates our awareness to appreciate our divine nature and perceive our interconnectedness with God. Ryuho Okawa bestows an enlightened perspective that peers beyond religious, political, societal, economic and academic disparities to mend the ambiguities of worldly conflict and reinforce God's infinite love.

LOVE FOR THE FUTURE
BUILDING ONE WORLD OF FREEDOM AND DEMOCRACY UNDER GOD'S TRUTH

Paperback • 312 pages • $15.95
ISBN: 978-1-942125-60-0 (Sep. 7, 2019)

This is a compilation of select international lectures given by Ryuho Okawa during his (ongoing) global missionary tours. While conflicting values of justice exist, this book espouses freedom and democracy are vital principles for global unification that will resolutely foster peace and shared prosperity, if adopted universally.

THE REASON WE ARE HERE
MAKE OUR POWERS TOGETHER TO REALIZE GOD'S JUSTICE -CHINA ISSUE, GLOBAL WARMING, AND LGBT-

Paperback • 215 pages • $14.95
ISBN: 978-1-943869-62-6 (Mar. 1, 2020)

The Reason We Are Here is a book of thought that is unlike any other: its global perspective, timely opinion on current issues, and spiritual class are unmatched. The main content is the lecture in Toronto, Canada given in October 2019 by Ryuho Okawa, a Japanese spiritual leader and the national teacher of Japan. Also included are his answers to the questions—specifically, on the Hong Kong and Uyghur problems—from renowned activists who attended his lecture.

For a complete list of books, visit okawabooks.com

GUIDANCE FROM SPACE IN THE AGE OF CRISIS

SPIRITUAL MESSAGES FROM YAIDRON
SAVE THE WORLD FROM DESTRUCTION

Paperback • 190 pages • $11.95
ISBN: 978-1-943928-23-1 (Dec. 25, 2021)

In this book, Yaidron explains what was going on behind the military coup in Myanmar and Taliban's control over Afghanistan. He also warns of the imminent danger approaching Taiwan. According to what he observes from the universe, World War III has already begun on Earth. What is now going on is a battle between democratic values and the communist one-party control. How to overcome this battle and create peace on Earth depends on the faith and righteous actions of each one of us.

SPIRITUAL MESSAGES FROM METATRON
LIGHT IN THE TIMES OF CRISIS

Paperback • 146 pages • $11.95
ISBN: 978-1-943928-19-4 (Nov. 4, 2021)

Metatron is one of the highest-ranking angels (seraphim) in Judaism and Christianity, and also one of the saviors of universe who has guided the civilizations of many planets including Earth, under the guidance of Lord God. Such savior has sent a message upon seeing the crisis of Earth. You will also learn about the truth behind the coronavirus pandemic, the unimaginable extent of China's desire, the danger of appeasement policy toward China, and the secret of Metatron.

R. A. GOAL'S WORDS FOR THE FUTURE

MESSAGES FROM A SPACE BEING
TO THE PEOPLE OF EARTH

Paperback • 174 pages • $11.95
ISBN: 978-1-943928-10-1 (Jun. 22, 2021)

R. A. Goal, a certified messiah from Planet Andalucia Beta in Ursa Minor, gives humans on Earth three predictions for 2021. They include the prospect of the novel coronavirus pandemic, the outlook of economic crisis, and the risk of war. But the hope is that Savior is now born on Earth to overcome any bad predictions. Now is the time to open our hearts and listen to the words from R. A. Goal.

For a complete list of books, visit okawabooks.com

PRESIDENT PUTIN AND THE FUTURE OF RUSSIA
An Interview with the Guardian Spirit of Vladimir Putin

PUTIN'S INSIGHTS ON RUSSIA, JAPAN AND THE WORLD
An Interview with the Guardian Spirit of the President of Russia

THE DESCENT OF ELOHIM
Spiritual Messages for the Movie, *The Laws of the Universe - The Age of Elohim*

THE LAWS OF FAITH
One World Beyond Differences

THE LAWS OF MISSION
Essential Truths for Spiritual Awakening in a Secular Age

THE LAWS OF STEEL
Living a Life of Resilience, Confidence and Prosperity

WITH SAVIOR
Messages from Space Being Yaidron

SHAKYAMUNI BUDDHA'S FUTURE PREDICTION
Including Spiritual Interview with John Lennon and Messages from Metatron and Yaidron

---

For a complete list of books, visit okawabooks.com

MUSIC BY RYUHO OKAWA

El Cantare Ryuho Okawa Original Songs

A song celebrating Lord God

A song celebrating Lord God, the God of the Earth, who is beyond a prophet.

The Water Revolution

English and Chinese version

For the truth and happiness of the 1.4 billion people in China who have no freedom. Love, justice, and sacred rage of God are on this melody that will give you courage to fight to bring peace.

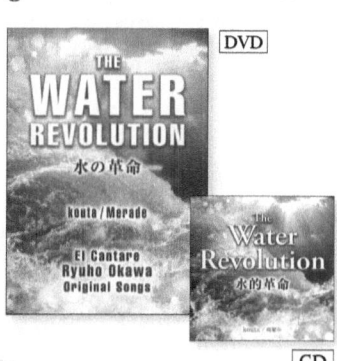

Search on YouTube

the water revolution 🔍 for a short ad!

Listen now today!

 Download from
Spotify   iTunes   Amazon

DVD, CD available at amazon.com, and Happy Science locations worldwide

With Savior *English version*

This is the message of hope to the modern people who are living in the midst of the Coronavirus pandemic, natural disasters, economic depression, and other various crises.

Search on YouTube

| with savior | for a short ad!

The Thunder
a composition for repelling the Coronavirus

We have been granted this music from our Lord. It will repel away the novel Coronavirus originated in China. Experience this magnificent powerful music.

Search on YouTube

| the thunder composition |

for a short ad!

The Exorcism
prayer music for repelling Lost Spirits

Feel the divine vibrations of this Japanese and Western exorcising symphony to banish all evil possessions you suffer from and to purify your space!

Search on YouTube

| the exorcism repelling |

for a short ad!

Listen now today!

 Download from **Spotify   iTunes   Amazon**

DVD, CD available at amazon.com, and Happy Science locations worldwide

www.ingramcontent.com/pod-product-compliance
Lightning Source LLC
Chambersburg PA
CBHW030150100526
44592CB00009B/202